AMERICAN VIRTUES,
VALUES & TRIUMPHS

PUBLICATIONS INTERNATIONAL, LTD.

⚓

CONTRIBUTING EDITORS:

Martha Cluverius Brown is a freelance writer whose work has appeared in such publications as *American Heritage* and *American History Illustrated*. She has a master's degree in English from Purdue University and is a former college and high school English teacher.

Bill Kauffman is the author of three books: *Every Man a King, Country Towns of New York*, and *America First!: Its History, Culture, and Politics*. He currently serves as Associate Editor of *American Enterprise* magazine, and he has written for *The American Scholar*, the *Los Angeles Times Book Review, Chronicles, The Nation, Liberty*, and many other periodicals.

Lucas E. Morel has a Ph.D. in political science. He is Assistant Professor of Political Science and History at Arkansas' John Brown University, where he teaches courses in American studies, political thought, and American government. He is currently at work on a book about the role of religion in Abraham Lincoln's statesmanship.

Publications International has made every effort to locate the owners of all copyrighted material to obtain permission to use the selections that appear in this book. Any errors or omissions are unintentional; corrections, if necessary, will be made in future editions.

ACKNOWLEDGEMENTS

page 26: Excerpt from A MIRROR FOR THE SKY, copyright ©1948 and renewed 1976 by Jessamyn West, reprinted by permission of Harcourt Brace & Company.

page 45: Excerpt from SAM WALTON: MADE IN AMERICA by Sam Walton. Copyright ©1992 by Estate of Samuel Moore Walton. Used by permission of Doubleday, a division of Bantam Doubleday Dell Publishing Group, Inc.

page 60: "A Marriage, An Elegy" from THE COLLECTED POEMS, 1957–1982 by Wendell Berry. Copyright ©1984 by Wendell Berry. Reprinted by permission of North Point Press, a division of Farrar, Straus & Giroux, Inc.

pages 62–63: Excerpt from SHANE. Copyright 1949, © renewed 1976 by Jack Schaefer. Reprinted by Houghton Mifflin Company. All rights reserved.

page 98: "i thank You God for most this amazing", copyright 1950, © 1978, 1991 by the Trustees for the E. E. Cummings Trust. Copyright © 1979 by George James Firmage, from COMPLETE POEMS: 1904–1962 by E. E. Cummings, Edited by George J. Firmage. Reprinted by permission of Liveright Publishing Corporation.

page 127: "It Couldn't Be Done" reprinted from THE COLLECTED VERSE OF EDGAR GUEST ©1934. Used with permission of Contemporary Books, Inc., Chicago.

page 164: "The Wizard of Oz" ©1939 Turner Entertainment Co. "The Wizard of Oz" and all related characters and elements are trademarks of Turner Entertainment Co. All rights reserved. Excerpts reprinted by permission of Turner Entertainment, Co.

page 213: Brief excerpt from LETTERS OF E.B. WHITE, collected and edited by Dorothy Lobrano Guth. Copyright © 1976 by E.B. White. Reprinted by permission of HarperCollins Publishers, Inc.

PHOTO CREDITS

Contents

Introduction

For those who appreciate the written word in all of its many forms, *American Virtues, Values & Triumphs* is a book that will provide hours of reading pleasure. Contained within these pages is a varied assortment of writings that celebrate and, at the same time, promote our best qualities as Americans—

and as individual human beings. The list includes poems, speeches, letters, song lyrics, short stories, anecdotes, and proverbs. Some of the selections are historical; some are literary. Some will make you laugh; others will surely bring a tear to your eye. Some will appeal to children; some will appeal to adults. Truly, there is something here for everyone.

As varied as the contents are, so too are the book's contributors, who represent all walks of life and all fields of endeavor. What they have in common is that, by stroke of luck or stroke of genius, they have

contributed to our collective consciousness because they had something thought-provoking, amusing, or otherwise memorable to say about life in this country or life in general.

To organize such a diverse collection of material, the book is divided into ten chapters, each representing one virtue or attribute as its theme: faith, courage, honesty, loyalty, freedom, perseverance, friendship, ingenuity, compassion, and humor. While these attributes are by no means exclusive to the American people, it is the purpose of this book to examine these qualities from a uniquely American perspective.

Note also that the arrangement of chapters and their contents is for the most part arbitrary, as each selection is intended to stand on its own.

Obviously, then, this is not a book that must be read from cover to cover. Rather, it invites endless browsing, be it to discover new favorites or to reread the old ones. That, in large part, is what makes this a book to be treasured—and a book worth sharing with others.

Freedom

Freedom is a beautiful word in any language, but it hasn't always meant what it means to us today. Throughout most of the world's history, it was a luxury reserved for those with wealth and power.

What was new and astonishing about the freedom that took root in American soil and inspired the authors of the Constitution was the notion that ordinary men and women had a natural, God-given right to speak, act, and worship as they saw fit. It was a notion our forebears were willing to fight and die for, even though the odds of success seemed overwhelmingly stacked against them at the time.

"Tyranny, like hell, is not easily conquered," patriot Thomas Paine cautioned in 1776. "Heaven knows how to put a proper price on its goods; and it would be strange indeed if so celestial an article as Freedom should not be highly rated."

Americans have paid the price gladly, making freedom the cornerstone upon which this nation was built. It has made possible the tremendous successes that we have achieved, and it serves as an example to the world that, as playwright Robert Sherwood put it, "Nothing undertaken by free men and free women is impossible."

These are the times that try men's souls. The summer soldier and the sunshine patriot will, in this crisis, shrink from the service of their country; but he that stands it now, deserves the love and thanks of man and woman. Tyranny, like hell, is not easily conquered; yet we have this consolation with us, that the harder the conflict, the more glorious the triumph. What we obtain too cheap, we esteem too lightly: It is dearness only that gives every thing its value. Heaven knows how to put a proper price upon its goods; and it would be strange indeed if so celestial an article as Freedom should not be highly rated.

—THOMAS PAINE, FROM THE FIRST OF HIS "AMERICAN CRISIS" PAPERS, PUBLISHED ON DECEMBER 19, 1776. FACING POSSIBLE DEFEAT, GEORGE WASHINGTON ORDERED THAT THE PAMPHLET BE READ TO HIS TROOPS AT VALLEY FORGE.

Released from imprisonment in Iran, American hostages arrive at West Germany's Rhein-Main Air Base on January 21, 1981.

To arms, then to arms! — 't is fair freedom invites us;
The trumpet shrill sounding, to battle excites us;
The banners of virtue unfurled shall wave o'er us,
Our heroes lead on, and the foe fly before us.

On Heaven and Washington placing reliance,
We'll meet the bold Briton, and bid him defiance;
Our cause we'll support, for 't is just and 't is glorious —
When men fight for freedom, they must be victorious.

—FROM "CAMP BALLAD," BY JOSEPH HOPKINSON (1777)

There are more instances of the abridgement of the freedom of the people by gradual and silent encroachments of those in power than by violent and sudden usurpation.

—JAMES MADISON (1751–1836)

In a government bottomed on the will of all, the liberty of every individual citizen becomes interesting to all.

—THOMAS JEFFERSON, FROM HIS FIFTH
ANNUAL PRESIDENT'S MESSAGE, 1805

This nation has placed its destiny in the hands and heads and hearts of its millions of free men and women; and its faith in freedom under the guidance of God. Freedom means the supremacy of human rights everywhere. Our support goes to those who struggle to gain those rights or keep them. Our strength is our unity of purpose.

To that high concept there can be no end save victory.

—FRANKLIN DELANO ROOSEVELT, FROM HIS 1941 MESSAGE TO CONGRESS

Experience has taught me belatedly that a farm begins with its fence. It keeps your own cattle out of your neighbor's fields and his out of yours. A fence is a definition and what it helps to define is that ownership of property which is the final guarantee of freedom. It cannot be breached without breaching freedom, and if it is ended, freedom is ended. Property is the ultimate guarantor of freedom. The benevolence of those who would deny this has nothing to do with the case. And earth is the ultimate property, of which every inch is, at need, a last ditch of freedom. In this sense, I worked for it and held it for you. In this sense, I give it to you and counsel you to hold it if you can.

—WHITTAKER CHAMBERS, A FORMER COMMUNIST WHO WAS THE STAR WITNESS AGAINST SOVIET SPY ALGER HISS, WRITING TO HIS SON

Now one of the most essential branches of English liberty is the freedom of one's house. A man's house is his castle; and whilst he is quiet, he is as well guarded as a prince in his castle.

—FROM A SPEECH BY JAMES OTIS, PRESENTED IN 1761, IN WHICH THE STATESMAN ARGUED AGAINST THE USE OF "WRITS" BY BRITISH TROOPS TO CONDUCT SEARCHES OF COLONISTS' HOMES AND BUSINESSES

THE GETTYSBURG ADDRESS

On November 19, 1863, an audience of approximately 15,000 people gathered at the little Pennsylvania town of Gettysburg to commemorate a cemetery for Civil War soldiers. The featured speaker for the ceremony was a popular orator named Edward Everett, whose long-winded presentation—filled with literary allusions, flowery verbiage, and frequent parenthetical departures—lasted for two long hours. When it was finally over, President Lincoln got up from his chair to make a brief concluding statement. Containing only 268 words, his speech took just over two minutes to deliver. Newspapers covering the ceremonies that day took little notice of it, and even the President thought he had made a poor showing. Today, the Gettysburg Address is considered one of the greatest Amercian speeches of all time.

Four score and seven years ago, our fathers brought forth upon this continent a new nation: conceived in liberty, and dedicated to the proposition that all men are created equal.

Now we are engaged in a great civil war... testing whether that nation, or any nation so conceived and so dedicated... can long endure. We are met on a great battlefield of that war.

We have come to dedicate a portion of that field as a final resting place for those who here gave their lives that this nation might live. It is altogether fitting and proper that we should do this.

But, in a larger sense, we cannot dedicate... we cannot consecrate... we cannot hallow this ground. The brave men, living and dead, who struggled here have consecrated it, far above our poor power to add or detract. The world will little note, nor long remember, what we say here, but it can never forget what they did here.

It is for us the living, rather, to be dedicated here to the unfinished work which they who fought here have thus far so nobly advanced. It is rather for us to be here dedicated to the great task remaining before us... that from these honored dead we take increased devotion to that cause for which they gave the last full measure of devotion... that we here highly resolve that these dead shall not have died in vain... that this nation, under God, shall have a new birth of freedom... and that government of the people... by the people... for the people... shall not perish from this earth.

My Country, 'tis of Thee

My country, 'tis of thee,
    Sweet land of liberty,
    Of thee I sing;
Land where my fathers died,
Land of the Pilgrims' pride,
From every mountain-side
    Let Freedom ring.

My native county, thee,
Land of the noble free —
    Thy name I love;
I love thy rocks and rills,
Thy woods and templed hills:
My heart with rapture thrills
    Like that above.

Let music swell the breeze,
And ring from all the trees
    Sweet Freedom's song;
Let mortal tongues awake,
Let all that breathe partake,
Let rocks their silence break —
    The sound prolong.

Our fathers' God, to Thee,
Author of liberty,
    To Thee we sing;
Long may our land be bright
With Freedom's holy light;
Protect us by Thy might,
    Great God, our King.

—Baptist clergyman and poet Samuel
Francis Smith (1808–1895)

This American government—what is it but a tradition, though a recent one, endeavoring to transmit itself unimpaired to posterity, but each instant losing some of its integrity? It has not the vitality and force of a single living man; for a single man can bend it to his will. It is a sort of wooden gun to the people themselves. But it is not the less necessary for this; for the people must have some complicated machinery or other, and hear its din, to satisfy that idea of government which they have. Governments show thus how successfully men can be imposed on, even impose on themselves, for their own advantage. It is excellent, we must all allow.

Yet this government never of itself furthered any enterprise, but by the alacrity with which it got out of its way. It does not keep the country free. It does not settle the West. It does not educate. The character inherent in the American people has done all that has been accomplished; and it would have done somewhat more, if the government had not sometimes got in its way. For government is an expedient by which men would fain succeed in letting one another alone; and, as has been said, when it is most expedient, the governed are most let alone by it.

—HENRY DAVID THOREAU, FROM "CIVIL DISOBEDIENCE" (1849)

Ay, this is freedom!—these pure skies
    Were never stained with village smoke:
The fragrant wind; that through them flies,
    Is breathed from wastes by plough unbroke.
Here, with my rifle and my steed,
    And her who left the world for me,
I plant me, where the red deer feed
    In the green desert—and am free.

Broad are these streams—my steed obeys,
    Plunges, and bears me through the tide.
Wide are these woods—I thread the maze
    Of giant stems, nor ask a guide.
I hunt till day's last glimmer dies
    O'er woody vale and grassy height;
And kind the voice and glad the eyes
    That welcome my return at night.

—WILLIAM CULLEN BRYANT (1794–1878), FROM "THE HUNTER OF THE PRAIRIES"

Benjamin Franklin

Benjamin Franklin said to Thomas Paine: "Where liberty is, there is my country." Paine answered, "Where liberty is not, there is mine."

—FROM *THE LITTLE, BROWN BOOK OF ANECDOTES*

Thomas Paine

The liberties of our country, the freedom of our civil constitution, are worth defending at all hazards; and it is our duty to defend them against all attacks. We have received them as a fair inheritance from our worthy ancestors: They purchased them for us with toil and danger and expense of treasure and blood, and transmitted them to us with care and diligence. It will bring an everlasting mark of infamy on the present generation, enlightened as it is, if we should suffer them to be wrested from us by violence without a struggle, or be cheated out of them by the artifices of false and designing men. Of the latter we are in most danger at present; let us therefore be aware of it. Let us contemplate our forefathers and posterity; and resolve to maintain the rights bequeathed to us from the former, for the sake of the latter.—Instead of sitting down satisfied with the efforts we have already made, *which is the wish of our enemies,* the necessity of the times, more than ever, calls for our utmost circumspection, deliberation, fortitude, and perseverance.

—SAMUEL ADAMS (1722–1803)

American suffragette parade in New York City, May 1912. It would take another eight years until the 19th Amendment would be passed, granting women the right to vote on an equal basis with men.

Is life so dear, or peace so sweet, as to be purchased at the price of chains and slavery? Forbid it, Almighty God! I know not what course others may take, but as for me, give me liberty, or give me death!

—LONG ATTRIBUTED TO REVOLUTIONARY WAR PATRIOT PATRICK HENRY, THIS FAMOUS QUOTE MAY ACTUALLY HAVE BEEN PENNED BY WILLIAM WIRT, HENRY'S BIOGRAPHER

The Americans were once scattered all over Europe. Here they are incorporated into one of the finest systems of population which has ever appeared and which will hereafter become distinct by the power of the different climates they inhabit. The American ought therefore to love this country much better than that in which either he or his fore-fathers were born. Here the rewards of his industry follow with equal steps the progress of his labor. His labor is founded on the basis of nature, *self-interest*: can it want a stronger allurement? Wives and children, who before in vain demanded of him a morsel of bread, now, fat and frolicsome, gladly help their father to clear those fields whence exuberant crops are to rise, to feed and to clothe them all, without any part being claimed either by a despotic prince, a rich abbot, or a mighty lord.

—FROM *LETTERS FROM AN AMERICAN FARMER* (1782), BY
J. HECTOR ST. JOHN DE CRÈVECOEUR (1735–1813)

Artist's rendering of the so-called Boston Tea Party, which took place on December 16, 1773.

The waves that wrought a century's wreck
    Have rolled o'er whig and tory;
The Mohawks on the Dartmouth's deck
    Still live in song and story;
The waters in the rebel bay
    Have kept the tea-leaf savor;

Our old North-Enders in their spray
    Still taste a Hyson* flavor;
And Freedom's teacup still o'erflows
    With ever fresh libations,
To cheat of slumber all her foes
    And cheer the wakening nations!

—OLIVER WENDELL HOLMES (1809–1894), FROM
"A BALLAD OF THE BOSTON TEA-PARTY"

* a type of tea popular during colonial times

Whereas, the Men of 1776 rebelled against the government which did not claim to be of the people, but on the contrary upheld the divine right of kings; and whereas, The women of this nation today, under a government which claims to be based upon individual rights, in an infinitely greater degree are suffering all the wrongs which led to the war of the Revolution; and whereas, The oppression is all the more keenly felt because our masters, instead of dwelling in a foreign land, are our husbands, fathers, brothers, sons; therefore,

Resolved, That the women of this nation, in 1876, have greater cause for discontent, rebellion and revolution than the men of 1776.

Resolved, That with Abigail Adams we believe "the passion for liberty cannot be strong in the breasts of those who are accustomed to deprive their fellow-creatures of liberty"; that, as she predicted in 1776, "we are determined to ferment a rebellion and will not be held bound by laws in which we have no voice nor representation."

—From Susan B. Anthony's "Declaration of Women's Rights," presented in 1876 at the Centennial of the Declaration of Independence

Engraving from *Harper's*, 1881.

SONG OF THE SETTLERS

Freedom is a hard-bought thing—
A gift no man can give,
For some, a way of dying,
For most, a way to live.

Freedom is a hard-bought thing—
A rifle in the hand,
The horses hitched at sunup,
A harvest in the land.

Freedom is a hard-bought thing—
A massacre, a bloody rout,
The candles lit at nightfall,
And the night shut out.

Freedom is a hard-bought thing—
An arrow in the back,
The wind in the long corn rows,
And the hay in the rack.

Freedom is a way of living,
A song, a mighty cry.
Freedom is the bread we eat;
Let it be the way we die!

—JESSAMYN WEST

The name of American, which belongs to you in your national capacity, must always exalt the just pride of patriotism more than any appellation derived from local discriminations. With slight shades of difference, you have the same religion, manners, habits, and political principles. You have in a common cause fought and triumphed together. The independence and liberty you possess are the work of joint councils and joint efforts, of common dangers, sufferings, and successes.

—GEORGE WASHINGTON, FROM HIS FAREWELL ADDRESS IN 1796

If we wish to be free; if we mean to preserve inviolate those inestimable privileges for which we have been so long contending; if we mean not basely to abandon the noble struggle in which we have been so long engaged, and which we have pledged ourselves never to abandon until the glorious object of our contest shall be obtained—we must fight! I repeat it, sir, we must fight! An appeal to arms, and to the God of hosts, is all that is left us.

—PATRICK HENRY (1736–1799)

In this unconquerably and justifiably optimistic nation nothing undertaken by free men and free women is impossible.

—PLAYWRIGHT ROBERT E. SHERWOOD (1896–1955)

It is my earnest hope—indeed the hope of all mankind—that from this solemn occasion a better world shall emerge out of the blood and carnage of the past. A world founded upon faith and understanding, a world dedicated to the dignity of man and the fulfillment of his most cherished wish for freedom, tolerance and justice.... Let us pray that peace be now restored to the world and that God will preserve it always. These proceedings are now closed.

—GENERAL DOUGLAS MACARTHUR, ACCEPTING THE JAPANESE
SURRENDER ABOARD THE U.S.S. *MISSOURI* ON SEPTEMBER 2, 1945

TO AN ANXIOUS FRIEND

Kansas newspaper editor William Allen White (1868–1944) wrote the following editorial for his newspaper, the Emporia Gazette, *in response to the repressive measures used by both state and federal governments to break the widespread railroad strike of 1922. Questionable injunctions made it illegal for strikers to picket—or even to discuss the issues of the strike.*

You tell me that law is above freedom of utterance. And I reply that you can have no wise laws nor free enforcement of wise laws until there is free expression of the wisdom of the people—and, alas, their folly with it. But if there is freedom, folly will die of its own poison, and the wisdom will survive. That is the history of the race. It is the proof of Man's kinship with God. You say that freedom of utterance is not for time of stress, and I reply with the sad truth that only in time of stress is freedom of utterance in danger. No one questions it in calm days, because it is not needed. And the reverse is true also; only when free utterance is suppressed is it needed and when it is needed, it is most vital to justice. Peace is good. But if you are interested in peace through force and without discussion, that is to say, free utterance decently and in order—your interest in justice is slight. And peace without justice is tyranny, no matter how you may sugar coat it with expediency. This state today is in more danger from suppression than from violence, because, in the end, suppression leads to violence. Violence, indeed, is the child of suppression. Whoever pleads for justice helps to keep the peace; and whoever tramples upon the plea for justice, temperately made in the name of peace, only outrages peace and kills something fine in the heart of man which God put there when we got our manhood. When that is killed, brute meets brute on each side of the line.

So, dear friend, put fear out of your heart. This nation will survive, this state will prosper, the orderly business of life will go forward if only men can speak in whatever way given them to utter what their hearts hold—by voice, by posted card, by letter or by press. Reason never has failed men. Only force and repression have made the wrecks in the world.

Government has no right to control individual liberty, beyond what is necessary to the safety and well-being of society.

—SOUTH CAROLINA STATESMAN
JOHN C. CALHOUN (1782–1850)

The people are the only censors of their governors; and even their errors will tend to keep these to the true principles of their institution. To punish these errors too severely would be to suppress the only safeguard of the public liberty. The way to prevent these irregular interpositions of the people, is to give them full information of their affairs through the channel of the public papers, and to contrive that those papers should penetrate the whole mass of the people. The basis of our governments being the opinion of the people, the very first object should be to keep that right; and were it left to me to decide whether we should have a government without newspapers, or newspapers without a government, I should not hesitate a moment to prefer the latter. But I should mean that every man should receive those papers, and be capable of reading them.

—THOMAS JEFFERSON, FROM A LETTER DATED JANUARY 16, 1787

We, therefore, the representatives of the United States of America, in general congress assembled, appealing to the Supreme Judge of the world for the rectitude of our intentions, do, in the name and by authority of the good people of these colonies, solemnly publish and declare, that these united colonies are, and of right ought to be, free and independent states; that they are absolved from all allegiance to the British Crown, and that all political connection between them and the state of Great Britain is, and ought to be, totally dissolved; and that as free and independent states they have full power to levy war, conclude peace, contract alliances, establish commerce, and to do all other acts and things which independent states may of right do. And for the support of this declaration, with a firm reliance on the protection of Divine Providence, we mutually pledge to each other our lives, our fortunes, and our sacred honor.

—FROM THE DECLARATION OF INDEPENDENCE, COMPOSED IN 1775 BY THOMAS JEFFERSON, JOHN ADAMS, BENJAMIN FRANKLIN, ROGER SHERMAN, AND ROBERT R. LIVINGSTON

This was their lofty, and wise, and noble understanding of the justice of the Creator to His creatures. Yes, gentlemen, to *all* His creatures, to the whole great family of man. . . . They grasped not only the whole race of man then living, but they reached forward and seized upon the farthest posterity. . . . Wise statesmen as they were, they knew the tendency of prosperity to breed tyrants, and so they established these great self-evident truths, that when in the distant future some man, some faction, some interest, should set up the doctrine that none but rich men, or none but white men, were entitled to life, liberty, and the pursuit of happiness, their posterity might look up again to the Declaration of Independence and take courage to renew the battle which their fathers began.

—ABRAHAM LINCOLN, SPEAKING OF THE "FOUNDING FATHERS"; FROM CARL SANDBURG'S 1939 BIOGRAPHY OF THE FORMER PRESIDENT

Declaration of Independence by John Trumbull (1756–1843).

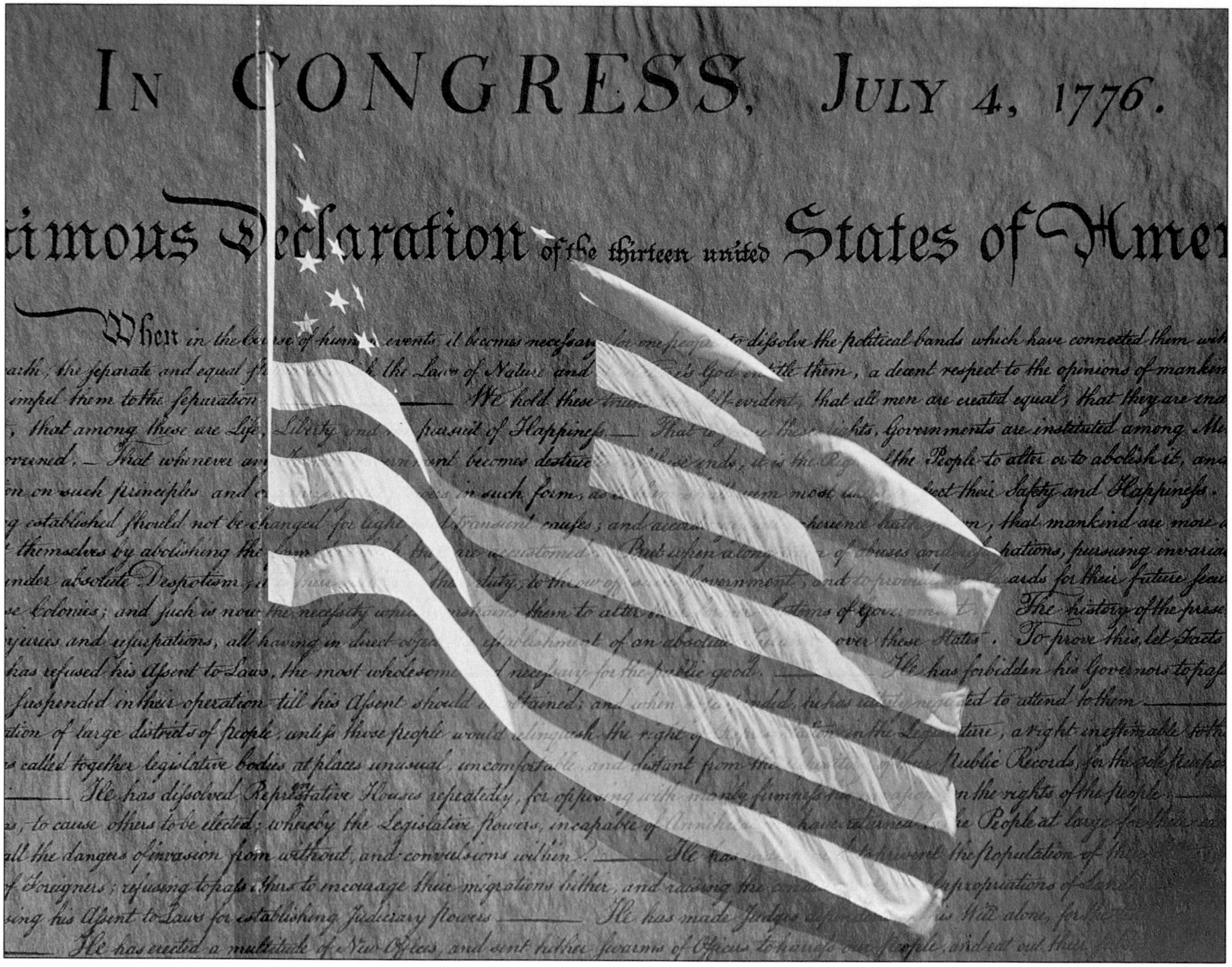
IN CONGRESS, JULY 4, 1776.
of the thirteen united States of

The Declaration of Independence! The interest which in that paper has survived the occasion upon which it was issued; the interest which is of every age and every clime; the interest which quickens with the lapse of years, spreads as it grows old, and brightens as it recedes, is in the principles which it proclaims.

It was the first solemn declaration, by a nation, of the only legitimate foundation of civil government. It was the corner stone of a new fabric, destined to cover the surface of the globe. It demolished at a stroke the lawfulness of all governments founded upon conquest. It swept away all the rubbish of accumulated centuries of servitude. It announced in practical form to the world the transcendent truth of the inalienable sovereignty of the people.

—JOHN QUINCY ADAMS (1767–1848)

THE AMERICAN'S CREED

I believe in the United States of America as a government of the people, by the people, for the people; whose just powers are derived from the consent of the governed; a democracy in a republic; a sovereign nation of many sovereign states; a perfect union, one and inseparable; established upon those principles of freedom, equality, justice, and humanity for which American patriots sacrificed their lives and fortunes. I therefore believe it is my duty to my country to love it, to support its constitution, to obey its laws, to respect its flag, and to defend it against all enemies.

—WILLIAM TYLER PAGE; ACCEPTED BY THE HOUSE OF REPRESENTATIVES ON APRIL 3, 1918.

Ingenuity

Physicist Albert Einstein, who believed that imagination was more important than knowledge, said that science is really "nothing more than a refinement of everyday thinking." As psychologist and philosopher William James put it, genius is simply "the faculty of perceiving in an unhabitual way."

Ingenuity enabled early Americans to survive and prosper in a strange land. It also established productive tinkering as a national trait. In the rest of the world, new inventions usually came from corporate or university laboratories; in the United States, they more often came from the toolsheds, kitchens, and garages of imaginative individuals.

Spurred by free enterprise, American inventors and entrepreneurs responded to the nation's hunger for progress and a better life. They developed ever more efficient farming implements to till the Great Plains, they harnessed electricity, they perfected the assembly line to mass-produce automobiles and countless other products, they built the first skyscrapers, and they pioneered in aviation and electronics.

Botanist George Washington Carver may have said it best: "When you can do the common things of life in an uncommon way, you will command the attention of the world."

A lot of people think that I have done things because of some "genius" that I've got. That . . . is not true. Any other bright-minded fellow can accomplish just as much if he will stick like hell and remember that nothing that's any good works by itself, just to please you; you got to make the damn thing work. You may have heard people repeat what I have said: "Genius is one percent inspiration, ninety-nine percent perspiration." Yes, sir, it's mostly hard work.

—Thomas Alva Edison
(1847–1931)

Never tell people how to do things. Tell them what to do, and they will surprise you with their ingenuity.

—General George S. Patton,
from *War As I Knew It* (1947)

If a man can write a better book, preach a better sermon, or make a better mouse-trap than his neighbor, though he builds his house in the woods, the world will make a beaten path to his door.

—Ralph Waldo Emerson, from an 1871 lecture

If a man be in advance of his age, he must be content to make his abode in [the Hall of Fantasy] until the lingering generations of his fellow-men come up with him. He can find no other shelter in the universe. But the fantasies of one day are the deepest realities of a future one.

—NATHANIEL HAWTHORNE (1804–1864), FROM *THE HALL OF FANTASY* (1846)

THE THINGS THAT HAVEN'T BEEN DONE BEFORE

The things that haven't been done before,
    Those are the things to try;
Columbus dreamed of an unknown shore
    At the rim of the far-flung sky,
And his heart was bold and his faith was strong
    As he ventured in dangers new,
And he paid no heed to the jeering throng
    Or the fears of the doubting crew.

The many will follow the beaten track
    With guideposts on the way,
They live and have lived for ages back
    With a chart for every day.
Someone has told them it's safe to go
    On the road he has traveled o'er,
And all that they ever strive to know
    Are the things that were known before.

A few strike out, without map or chart,
    Where never a man has been,
From the beaten paths they draw apart
    To see what no man has seen.
There are deeds they hunger alone to do;
    Though battered and bruised and sore,
They blaze the path for the many, who
    Do nothing not done before.

The things that haven't been done before
    Are the tasks worth while to-day;
Are you one of the flock that follows, or
    Are you one that shall lead the way?
Are you one of the timid souls that quail
    At the jeers of a doubting crew,
Or dare you, whether you win or fail,
    Strike out for a goal that's new?

—EDGAR A. GUEST (1881–1959)

Like his "muckers," Thomas Edison proudly punched in and out at the Laboratory every day. His time clock card for the week ending September 10, 1912, registered 111 hours, 48 minutes. "Say, we are working all night tonight," telephoned Edison's sidekick Fred Ott—nicknamed "Santcho Pantcho" by his self-styled Don Quixote boss—to young chemist M. A. Rosanoff. "The Old Man says to ask you if you want to come up to the lab." Rosanoff groaned under his breath, got out of bed, and dressed hurriedly. He found the factory brightly lit, Edison with son Charles at his side, and a group of assistants in attendance. "Say," Edison hailed the chemist, "let's you and I go to work on your damned problem [formulation of Aylsworth's hardened coating for the cylinders] to-night and make a resolution not to go to sleep until we have solved it!"

"Mr. Edison," Rosanoff pleaded, "you know I have been at my problem for months; I have tried every reasonable thing I could think of, and no result, not even a lead!"

"That's just where your trouble has been," the Old Man interrupted. "You have tried only reasonable things. Reasonable things never work. Thank God you can't think up any more reasonable things, so you'll have to begin thinking up *un*reasonable things to try, and now you'll hit the solution in no time. After that, you can take a nap," he added reassuringly.

— NEIL BALDWIN, FROM *EDISON: INVENTING THE CENTURY* (1995)

THE POST-IT NOTES™ STORY

Post-It Notes™ can be found in almost any office in the United States today, and they are a $200-million-a-year success for the 3M Corporation. But it did not come easy.

The idea originated with Art Fry, a 3M employee who used bits of paper to mark hymns when he sat in his church choir. These markers kept falling out of the hymn books. He decided that he needed an adhesive-backed paper that would stick as long as necessary but could be removed easily. He soon found what he wanted in the 3M laboratory, and the Post-It Note™ was born.

Fry saw the market potential of his invention, but others did not. Market-survey results were negative; major office-supply distributors were skeptical. So he began giving samples to 3M executives and their secretaries. Once they actually used the little pieces of adhesive paper, they were hooked. Having sold 3M on the project, Fry used the same approach with other executives throughout the United States. He mailed samples to the secretaries and CEOs of Fortune 500 firms. They soon became hooked, too. As demand grew, Post-It Notes™ became a huge financial success.

—JAMES M. HIGGINS, FROM *THE FUTURIST* (SEPT.–OCT. 1995)

Genius, in truth, means little more than the faculty of perceiving in an unhabitual way.

—PSYCHOLOGIST AND PHILOSOPHER WILLIAM JAMES (1842–1910)

Only an inventor knows how to borrow, and every man is or should be an inventor.

—RALPH WALDO EMERSON (1803–1882)

Nature, in its ministry to man, is not only the material, but is also the process and the result. All the parts incessantly work into each other's hands for the profit of man. The wind sows the seed; the sun evaporates the sea; the wind blows the vapor to the field; the ice, on the other side of the planet, condenses rain on this; the rain feeds the plant; the plant feeds the animal; and thus the endless circulations of the divine charity nourish man.

The useful arts are reproductions or new combinations by the wit of man, of the same natural benefactors. He no longer waits for favoring gales, but by means of steam, he realizes the fable of Aeolus's bag, and carries the two and thirty winds in the boiler of his boat. To diminish friction, he paves the road with iron bars, and, mounting a coach with a ship-load of men, animals, and merchandise behind him, he darts through the country, from town to town, like an eagle or a swallow through the air. By the aggregate of these aids, how is the face of the world changed, from the era of Noah to that of Napoleon! The private poor man hath cities, ships, canals, bridges, built for him.

—RALPH WALDO EMERSON, FROM *NATURE* (1849)

When you can do the common things of life in an uncommon way, you will command the attention of the world.

—BOTANIST GEORGE WASHINGTON CARVER
(1864–1943)

Nobel Prize award ceremony in Stockholm, Sweden. Established through the will of Swedish chemist and engineer Alfred Nobel (1833–1896), the Nobel Prize awards have been presented each year since 1901 "to those who, during the preceding year, shall have conferred the greatest benefit on mankind" in the fields of physics, chemistry, physiology or medicine, literature and peace. A prize for economics was initiated in 1968.

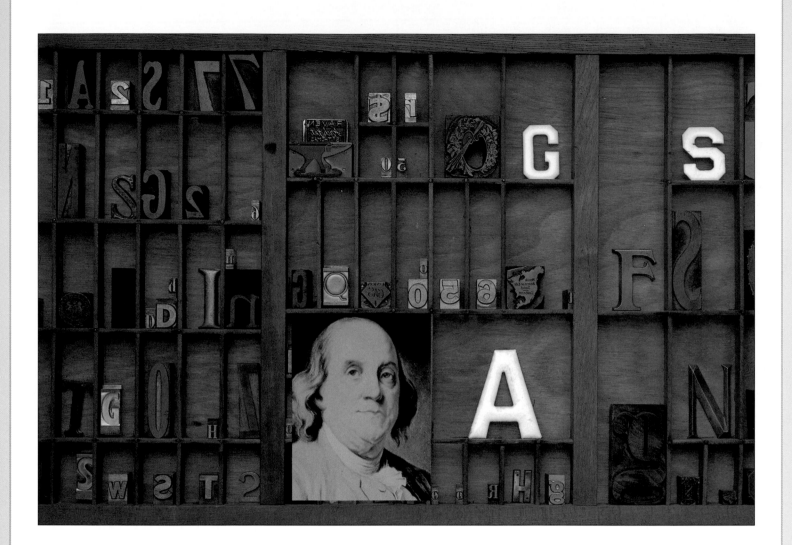

Having been apprenticed to a printer from the age of 12, Benjamin Franklin (1706–1790) became an expert in the field. During the course of his long and fruitful life, he would establish himself as a publisher, author, diplomat, and, as is evident from the following passage from his autobiography (published in 1793), an inventor and a scientist.

Our Printing-House often wanted Sorts, and there was no Letter Founder in America. I had seen Types cast at James's in London, but without much Attention to the Manner: However I now contriv'd a Mould, made use of the Letters we had, as Puncheons, struck the Matrices in Lead, and thus supply'd in a pretty tolerable way all Deficiencies. I also engrav'd several Things on occasion. I made the Ink, I was Warehouse-man & every thing, in short quite a Factotum.

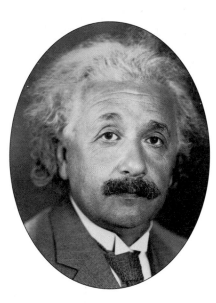

Right away I started looking around for store opportunities in other towns. Maybe it was just my itch to do more business, and maybe, too, I didn't want all my eggs in one basket again. By 1952 I had driven down to Fayetteville and found an old grocery store that Kroger was abandoning because it was falling apart. It was right on the square, only 18 feet wide and 150 feet deep. Our main competitor was a Woolworth's on one side of the square, and a Scott Store on the other side of the square. So here we were challenging two popular stores with a little old 18-foot independent variety store. It wasn't a Ben Franklin franchise; we just called it Walton's Five and Dime like the store in Bentonville. I remember sitting on the square right after I bought it listening to a couple of the local codgers say: "Well, we'll give that guy sixty days, maybe ninety. He won't be there long."

But this store was ahead of its time too, self-service all the way, unlike the competition. This was the beginning of our way of operating for a long while to come. We were innovating, experimenting, and expanding. Somehow over the years, folks have gotten the impression that Wal-Mart was something I dreamed up out of the blue as a middle-aged man, and that it was just this great idea that turned into an overnight success. It's true that I was forty-four when we opened our first Wal-Mart in 1962, but the store was totally an outgrowth of everything we'd been doing since Newport—another case of me being unable to leave well enough alone, another experiment. And like most other overnight successes, it was about twenty years in the making.

—Sam Walton, founder of Wal-Mart, from his autobiography
Made in America (with John Huey, 1992)

The whole of science is nothing more than a refinement of everyday thinking.

—Physicist Albert Einstein
(1879–1955)

What the socialists call the exploiter and capitalist is the modern representative and successor of a long line of inventors who have taught men frugality in some degree and made possible active leisure...over...savage apathy. Were the ingenuities of these inventors done away with, human life would be reduced once more to that of the raccoon—saving his honor.

—HISTORIAN JAMES HARVEY ROBINSON (1863–1936)

Daedalus was so proud of his achievements that he could not bear the idea of a rival. His sister had placed her son Perdix under his charge to be taught the mechanical arts. He was an apt scholar and gave striking evidences of ingenuity. Walking on the seashore he picked up the spine of a fish. Imitating it, he took a piece of iron and notched it on the edge, and thus invented the saw. He put two pieces of iron together, connecting them at one end with a rivet, and sharpening the other ends, and made a pair of compasses.

Daedalus was so envious of his nephew's performances that he took an opportunity, when they were together one day on the top of a high tower, to push him off. But Minerva, who favours ingenuity, saw him falling, and arrested his fate by changing him into a bird called after his name, the Partridge. This bird does not build his nest in the trees, nor take lofty flights, but nestles in the hedges, and mindful of his fall, avoids high places.

—Thomas Bulfinch (1796–1867),
from *The Age of Fables* (1855)

Men say they know many things;
But lo! they have taken wings,
The arts and sciences,
And a thousand appliances:
The wind that blows
Is all that anybody knows.

—Henry David Thoreau,
from *Walden* (1854)

Back in 1869, someone asked Samuel Sparks Fisher, Commissioner of Patents, what proportion of patented inventions were truly useful. His reply:

Probably not much more than one-tenth; but let it be remembered, there are few failures so harmless as that of a useless invention. The patent gives it a chance to prove itself worthy of the public patronage. It simply declares that if it be good it shall not be stolen. But if it be useless, nobody would *want* to steal it.

—From *The Art of Invention: Patents, Models, and Their Makers*, by William and Marlys Ray (1974)

Inventors must be poets so that they may have imagination.

—Thomas Alva Edison
(1847–1931)

This motorized roller skate, invented by M. Mercier earlier this century, was fitted with a two-cylinder (one-quarter-horsepower) motor that could generate a speed of 20 miles per hour. Perhaps ahead of its time, the product never took off.

He who invents a machine augments the power of a man and the well-being of mankind.

—Clergyman Henry Ward Beecher (1813–1887)

BROOKLYN BRIDGE

Considered an incredible feat of engineering when it was completed in 1883 after 14 years of construction, the Brooklyn Bridge was the first to use cable wire made of steel and until 1890 boasted the longest main span (1,595 feet) of any bridge in the world.

No lifeless thing of iron and stone,
　　But sentient, as her children are,
Nature accepts you for her own,
　　Kin to the cataract and the star.

She marks your vast, sufficing plan,
　　Cable and girder, bolt and rod,
And takes you, from the hand of man,
　　For some new handiwork of God.

You thrill through all your chords of steel
　　Responsive to the living sun;
And quickening in your nerves you feel
　　Life with its conscious currents run.

Your anchorage upbears the march
　　Of time and the eternal powers.
The sky admits your perfect arch,
　　The rock respects your stable towers.

—CHARLES G. D. ROBERTS (1860–1943)

Although often portrayed as solemn and conservative, George Washington displayed plenty of ingenuity as a military commander. Consider the following excerpt from A Message to Garcia *(1916), by Elbert Hubbard.*

At Princeton, Washington ordered campfires to be built along the brow of a hill for a mile, and when the fires were well lighted, he withdrew his army, marched around to the other side, and surprised the enemy at daylight. At Brooklyn he used masked batteries, and presented a fierce row of round, black spots painted on canvas that, from the city, looked like the mouths of cannon at which men seek the bauble reputation. It is said he also sent a note threatening to fire these sham cannon, on receiving which the enemy hastily moved beyond range.

A fellow actress once said of Miss (Tallulah) Bankhead: "She's not so great. I can upstage her any time."

"Darling," retorted Tallulah, "I can upstage you without even being on stage." At the next performance, she set out to prove her point. In one scene, while the other actress was engrossed in a long telephone conversation, Tallulah had to put down the champagne glass from which she had been drinking and make her exit upstage. That evening, she carefully placed the half-full glass in a precarious position at the edge of the table, half on and half off. The audience gasped, their attention riveted to the glass, and the other actress was totally ignored. She later discovered that Miss Bankhead had surreptitiously stuck a piece of adhesive tape on the bottom of the glass to ensure the success of her moment of triumph.

—FROM *THE LITTLE, BROWN BOOK OF ANECDOTES* (LITTLE, BROWN & CO., 1985)

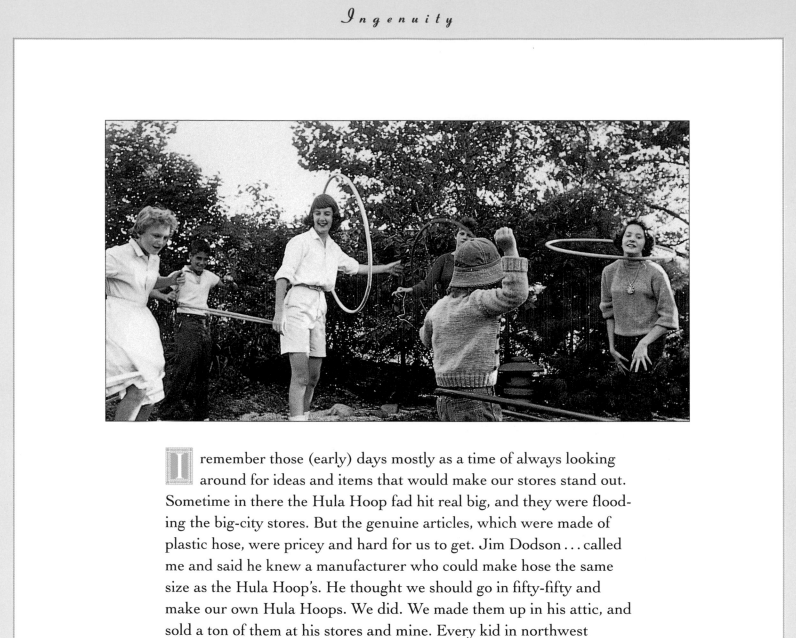

I remember those (early) days mostly as a time of always looking around for ideas and items that would make our stores stand out. Sometime in there the Hula Hoop fad hit real big, and they were flooding the big-city stores. But the genuine articles, which were made of plastic hose, were pricey and hard for us to get. Jim Dodson . . . called me and said he knew a manufacturer who could make hose the same size as the Hula Hoop's. He thought we should go in fifty-fifty and make our own Hula Hoops. We did. We made them up in his attic, and sold a ton of them at his stores and mine. Every kid in northwest Arkansas had to have one. Later Jim ended up managing a Wal-Mart for us up in Columbia, Missouri, for about fifteen years.

—SAM WALTON, FOUNDER OF WAL-MART, FROM HIS AUTOBIOGRAPHY
MADE IN AMERICA (WITH JOHN HUEY, 1992)

AMERICA'S FIRST LIBRARY

Among his many accomplishments, Benjamin Franklin is credited with establishing one of the country's first lending libraries. Philadelphia was the site; the year was 1730. Franklin explains how it was done in The Autobiography of Benjamin Franklin *(1793).*

I propos'd to render the Benefit from Books more common by commencing a Public Subscription Library. I drew a Sketch of the Plan and Rules that would be necessary, and got a skilful Conveyancer, Mr. Charles Brockden to put the whole in Form of Articles of Agreement to be subscribed; by which each Subscriber engag'd to pay a certain Sum down for the first Purchase of Books and an annual Contribution for encreasing them. So few were the Readers at that time in Philadelphia, and the Majority of us so poor, that I was not able with great Industry to find more than Fifty Persons, mostly young Tradesmen, willing to pay down for this purpose Forty shillings each, & Ten Shillings per Annum. On this little Fund we began. The Books were imported. The Library was open one Day in the Week for lending them to the Subscribers, on their Promisory Notes to pay Double the Value if not duly returned. The Institution soon manifested its Utility, was imitated by other Towns and in other Provinces, the Librarys were augmented by Donations, Reading became fashionable, and our People having no publick Amusements to divert their Attention from Study became better acquainted with Books, and in a few Years were observ'd by Strangers to be better instructed & more intelligent than People of the same Rank generally are in other Countries.

Friendship

A deep and abiding friendship may indeed be "a plant of slow growth," as George Washington once remarked, but few things in life are as treasured—and rightly so.

Ultimately, the greatest friendships—whether they occur between youngsters or a couple of lifelong friends grown gray—are based on mutual trust. "A friend is a person with whom I may be sincere," wrote essayist and poet Ralph Waldo Emerson, "and from that sincerity a thousand glories and pleasures flow."

"There is no friend like an old friend," offered author and physician Oliver Wendell Holmes. True enough, though Maine novelist Sarah Orne Jewett later amended the popular maxim: "Yes'm, old friends is always best, 'less you can catch a new one that's fit to make an old one out of."

Ty Cobb, famous for his talents at baseball, but not very good in his relationships with other people, said late in his life that the one thing he regretted was not having more friends. Even money and fame seem to be less fulfilling without the company of friends to share them with. Having friends may take some work, but the rewards are often immeasurable.

Observe good faith and justice toward all nations; cultivate peace and harmony with all. Religion and morality enjoin this conduct, and can it be that good policy does not equally enjoin it? It will be worthy of a free, enlightened, and, at no distant period, a great nation, to give to mankind the magnanimous and novel example of a people always guided by an exalted justice and benevolence.

—GEORGE WASHINGTON, FROM HIS FAREWELL ADDRESS, DELIVERED ON SEPTEMBER 19, 1796

Instead of loving your enemies, treat your friends a little better.

—JOURNALIST ED HOWE (1853–1937)

I awoke this morning with devout thanksgiving for my friends, the old and the new.

—RALPH WALDO EMERSON (1803–1882)

Sweet is the memory of distant friends!
Like the mellow rays of the departing sun,
it falls tenderly, yet sadly, on the heart.

—NOVELIST AND HISTORIAN WASHINGTON IRVING (1783–1859)

Soil and friendship must be cultivated.

—American proverb

A true friend unbosoms freely, advises justly, assists readily, adventures boldly, takes all patiently, defends courageously, and continues a friend unchangeably.

—William Penn (1644–1718), Quaker founder of Pennsylvania Colony

No man can be fully free while his neighbor is not. To go forward at all is to go forward together. This means black and white together, as one nation, not two.

—Richard Nixon, from his 1969 Inaugural Address

*I do not wish to treat friendships
daintily, but with roughest courage.
When they are real, they are not glass
threads or frostwork, but the solidest
thing we know.*

—RALPH WALDO EMERSON (1803–1882)

There are many kinds of fruit
that grow on the tree of life, but
none so sweet as friendship.

—AMERICAN PROVERB

The essence of friendship is not
getting, but sharing.

—AMERICAN PROVERB

A MARRIAGE, AN ELEGY

They lived long, and were faithful to the good in each other.
They suffered as their faith required.
Now their union is consummate
in earth, and the earth
is their communion. They enter
the serene gravity of the rain,
the hill's passage to the sea.
After long striving, perfect ease.

—WENDELL BERRY, FROM *COLLECTED POEMS 1957–1982*

A friend is a person with whom I may be sincere. Before him I may think aloud. I am arrived at last in the presence of a man so real and equal that I may drop even those undermost garments of dissimulation, courtesy, and second thought, which men never put off, and may deal with him with the simplicity and wholeness with which one chemical atom meets another.

—RALPH WALDO EMERSON (1803–1882)

Do good to thy friend to keep him, to thy enemy to gain him.

—BENJAMIN FRANKLIN
(1706–1790)

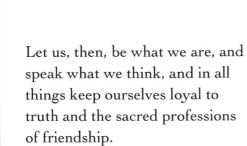

Let us, then, be what we are, and speak what we think, and in all things keep ourselves loyal to truth and the sacred professions of friendship.

—HENRY WADSWORTH
LONGFELLOW (1807–1882)

SHANE

I guess that is all there is to tell. The folks in town and the kids at school liked to talk about Shane, to spin tales and speculate about him. I never did. Those nights at Grafton's became legends in the valley and countless details were added as they grew and spread just as the town, too, grew and spread up the river banks. But I never bothered, no matter how strange the tales became in the constant retelling. He belonged to me, to father and mother and me, and nothing could ever spoil that.

For mother was right. He was there. He was there in our place and in us. Whenever I needed him, he was there. I could close my eyes and he would be with me and I would see him plain and hear again that gentle voice.

I would think of him in each of the moments that revealed him to me. I would think of him most vividly in that single flashing instant when he whirled to shoot Fletcher on the balcony at Grafton's saloon. I would see again the power and grace of a coordinate force beautiful beyond comprehension. I would see the man and the weapon wedded in the one indivisible deadliness. I would see the man and the tool, a good man and a good tool, doing what had to be done.

And always my mind would go back at the last to that moment when I saw him from the bushes by the roadside just on the edge of town. I would see him there in the road, tall and terrible in the moonlight, going down to kill or be killed, and stopping to help a stumbling boy and to look out over the land, the lovely land, where that boy had a chance to live out his boyhood and grow straight inside as a man should.

And when I would hear the men in town talking among themselves and trying to pin him down to a definite past, I would smile quietly to myself. For a time they inclined to the notion, spurred by the talk of a passing stranger, that he was a certain Shannon who was famous as a gunman and gambler way down in Arkansas and Texas and dropped from sight without anyone knowing why or where. When that notion dwindled, others followed, pieced together in turn from scraps of information gleaned from stray travelers. But when they talked like that, I simply smiled because I knew he could have been none of these.

He was the man who rode into our little valley out of the heart of the great glowing West and when his work was done rode back whence he had come and he was Shane.

—JACK SCHAEFER, FROM HIS 1949 NOVEL *SHANE*

Friendship is a magic weaver.

—AMERICAN PROVERB

The supreme need of our time is for men to learn to live together in peace and harmony.

—HARRY S TRUMAN, FROM HIS 1949 INAUGURAL ADDRESS

Let us then all labor for the unity of the nation by working for the education of its citizens, for the spread of virtue and true morality, for the promotion of our industry which will redeem the poor from servile and social drudgery, for the freedom of its commerce, for a more just and generous sympathy between all its races and classes, for a more benignant spirit to its religion; and finally, let us implore the God of our fathers, by his own wise providence, to save us from our wanton passions, from impertinent egotism, from pride, arrogance, cruelty, and sensual lusts, that as a nation we may show forth his praise in all the earth.

—CLERGYMAN HENRY WARD BEECHER (1813–1887), FROM A SERMON DELIVERED ON NOVEMBER 18, 1869

Never Explain—your Friends do not need it and your Enemies will not believe you anyway.

—WRITER AND EDITOR ELBERT HUBBARD (1856–1915)

Water your friendships as you water your flowerpots.

—AMERICAN PROVERB

Having defeated incumbent John Adams, a Federalist, in the Presidential election of 1800, Thomas Jefferson, a Republican, made the following plea for unity shortly after being sworn into office on March 4, 1801.

Let us then, fellow-citizens, unite with one heart and one mind, let us restore to social intercourse that harmony and affection without which liberty and even life itself are but dreary things. And let us reflect, that having banished from our land that religious intolerance under which mankind so long bled and suffered, we have yet gained little, if we countenance a political intolerance, as despotic, as wicked, and as capable of as bitter and bloody persecutions.

During the throes and convulsions of the ancient world, during the agonizing spasms of infuriated man, seeking through blood and slaughter his long-lost liberty, it was not wonderful that the agitation of the billows should reach even this distant and peaceful shore; that this should be more felt and feared by some, and less by others, and should divide opinions as to measures of safety; but every difference of opinion is not a difference of principle. We have called by different names brethren of the same principle. We are all Republicans; we are all Federalists.

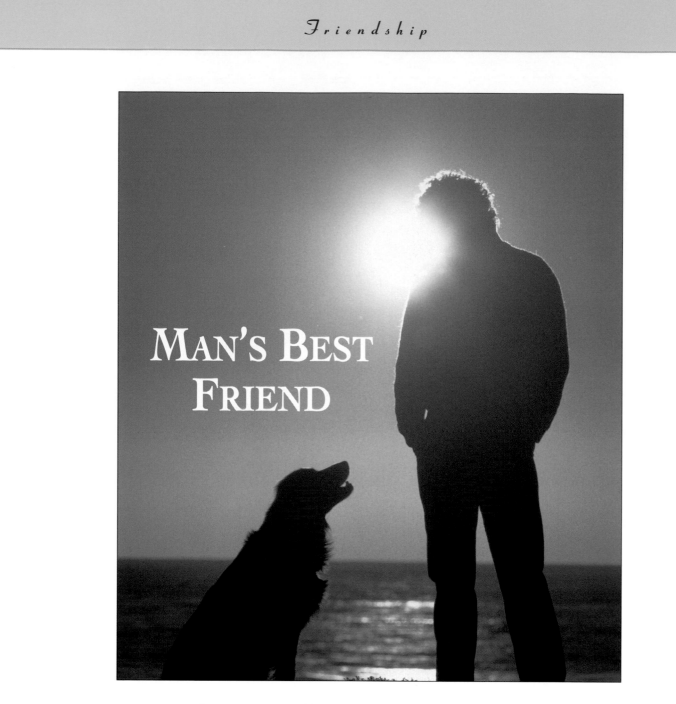

MAN'S BEST FRIEND

George Graham Vest had a distinguished political career, serving four consecutive six-year terms (1879–1903) as a Missouri senator. Outside of the state, he is best remembered—particularly among dog fanciers—for the following courtroom speech, made when he was a young lawyer representing a man who was suing another for killing his dog.

Gentlemen of the Jury: The best friend a man has in the world may turn against him and become his enemy. His son or daughter that he has reared with loving care may prove ungrateful. Those who are nearest and dearest to us, those whom we trust with our happiness and our good name may become traitors to their faith.

The money that a man has he may lose. It flies away from him, perhaps when he needs it most. A man's reputation may be sacrificed in a moment of ill-considered action. The people who are prone to fall on their knees when success is with us, may be the first to throw the stone of malice when failure settles its cloud upon our head.

The one absolutely unselfish friend that man can have in this selfish world, the one that never deserts him, the one that never proves ungrateful or treacherous, is his dog. A man's dog stands by him in prosperity and in poverty, in health and in sickness. He will sleep on the cold ground, where the wintry winds blow and the snow drives fiercely, if only he may be near his master's side. He will kiss the hand that has no food to offer; he will lick the wounds and sores that come in encounters with the roughness of the world. He guards the sleep of his pauper master as if he were a prince.

When all other friends desert, he remains. When riches take wings, and reputation falls to pieces, he is as constant in his love as the sun in its journey through the heavens.

If fortune drive his master forth an outcast in the world, friendless and homeless, the faithful dog asks no higher privilege than that of accompanying him, to guard him against danger, to fight against his enemies. And when the last scene of all comes, and death takes his master in its embrace and his body is laid away in the cold ground, no matter if all other friends pursue their way, there by the graveside will the noble dog be found, his head between his paws, his eyes sad, but open in alert watchfulness, faithful and true even in death.

We are not enemies, but friends. We must not be enemies. Though passion may have strained, it must not break our bonds of affection. The mystic chords of memory, stretching from every battlefield and patriot grave to every living heart and hearthstone all over this broad land, will yet swell the chorus of the Union, when again touched, as surely they will be, by the better angels of our nature.

—ABRAHAM LINCOLN, FROM HIS
1861 INAUGURAL ADDRESS

UP FROM SLAVERY

Excerpted from a speech by black educator Booker T. Washington at the 1895 Atlanta Exposition and later incorporated into his autobiography Up From Slavery *(1901).*

A ship lost at sea for many days suddenly sighted a friendly vessel. From the mast of the unfortunate vessel was seen a signal, "Water, water; we die of thirst!" The answer from the friendly vessel at once came back, "Cast down your bucket where you are." A second time the signal, "Water, water; send us water!" ran up from the distressed vessel, and was answered, "Cast down your bucket where you are." And a third and fourth signal for water was answered, "Cast down your bucket where you are." The captain of the distressed vessel, at last heeding the injunction, cast down his bucket, and it came up full of fresh, sparkling water from the mouth of the Amazon River.

To those of my race who depend on bettering their condition in a foreign land or who underestimate the importance of cultivating friendly relations with the Southern white man, who is their next-door neighbour, I would say: "Cast down your bucket where you are"—cast it down in making friends in every manly way of the people of all races by whom we are surrounded.

LET SOMETHING GOOD BE SAID

When over the fair fame of friend or foe
    The shadow of disgrace shall fall, instead
Of words of blame, or proof of thus and so,
    Let something good be said.

Forget not that no fellow-being yet
    May fall so low but love may lift his head:
Even the cheek of shame with tears is wet,
    If something good be said.

No generous heart may vainly turn aside
    In ways of sympathy; no soul so dead
But may awaken strong and glorified,
    If something good be said.

And so I charge ye, by the thorny crown,
    And by the cross on which the Saviour bled,
And by your own soul's hope of fair renown,
    Let something good be said!

    —JAMES WHITCOMB RILEY (1849–1916),
      KNOWN AS "THE HOOSIER POET"

Instead of gazing at each other with suspicious or doubtful curiosity, let each of us hold out to his neighbor the hearty hand of friendship, and unite in drawing a line, which, like an act of oblivion, shall bury in forgetfulness every former dissension. Let the names of Whig and Tory be extinct; and let none other be heard among us, than those of a good citizen; an open and resolute friend; and a virtuous supporter of the Rights of Mankind, and of the Free and Independent States of America.

    —THOMAS PAINE, FROM *COMMON SENSE* (1776)

Let us resolve that we the people will build an American opportunity society in which all of us—white and black, rich and poor, young and old—will go forward together arm in arm. Again, let us remember that though our heritage is one of blood lines from every corner of the Earth, we are all Americans pledged to carry on this last, best hope of man on Earth.

—RONALD REAGAN, FROM HIS
1985 INAUGURAL ADDRESS

John Adams

There still remains one effort of magnanimity, one sacrifice of prejudice and passion, to be made by the individuals throughout the nation who have heretofore followed the standards of political party. It is that of discarding every remnant of rancor against each other, of embracing as countrymen and friends, and of yielding to talents and virtue alone that confidence which in times of contention for principle was bestowed only upon those who bore the badge of party communion.

—JOHN QUINCY ADAMS, FROM HIS 1825 INAUGURAL ADDRESS

THREE FRIENDS OF MINE

When I remember them, those friends of mine,
   Who are no longer here, the noble three,
   Who half my life were more than friends to me,
   And whose discourse was like a generous wine,
I most of all remember the divine
   Something, that shone in them, and made us see
   The archetypal man, and what might be
   The amplitude of Nature's first design.

In vain I stretch my hands to clasp their hands;
   I cannot find them. Nothing now is left
   But a majestic memory. They meanwhile
Wander together in Elysian lands,
   Perchance remembering me, who am bereft
   Of their dear presence, and, remembering, smile.

—HENRY WADSWORTH LONGFELLOW (1807–1882)

While you seek new friendships, cultivate the old.

—AMERICAN PROVERB

Wherever you are, it is your own friends who make your world.

—PSYCHOLOGIST AND PHILOSOPHER
WILLIAM JAMES (1842–1910)

For memory has painted this perfect day
With colors that never fade,
And we find at the end of a perfect day
The soul of a friend we've made.

—CARRIE JACOBS BOND (1862–1946)

Even the death of friends will inspire us as much as their lives.... Their memories will be encrusted over with sublime and pleasing thoughts, as monuments of other men are overgrown with moss; for our friends have no place in the graveyard.

—HENRY DAVID THOREAU (1817–1862)

TENTING ON THE OLD CAMPGROUND

We're tenting tonight on the old
    campground,
Give us a song to cheer
Our weary hearts, a song
    of home
And friends we love so dear.

—WALTER KITTREDGE (1834–1905)

THE DAYS OF 'FORTY-NINE

The number forty-nine, as it is used in this once-popular poem,
refers to 1849, the year that the California Gold Rush began.

You are looking now on old Tom Moore,
    A relic of bygone days;
A Bummer, too, they call me now,
    But what care I for praise?
For my heart is filled with the days of yore,
    And oft I do repine
For the Days of Old, and the Days of Gold,
    And the Days of 'Forty-Nine.

I had comrades then who loved me well,
    A jovial, saucy crew:
There were some hard cases, I must confess,
    But they all were brave and true;
Who would never flinch, whate'er the pinch,
    Who never would fret nor whine,
But like good old Bricks they stood the kicks
    In the Days of 'Forty-Nine.

There was Monte Pete—I'll ne'er forget
    The luck he always had.
He would deal for you both day and night,
    So long as you had a scad.
He would play you Draw, he would Ante sling,
    He would go you a hatfull Blind—
But in a game with Death Pete lost his breath
    In the Days of 'Forty-Nine.

There was New York Jake, a butcher boy,
    That was always a-getting tight;
Whenever Jake got on a spree,
    He was spoiling for a fight.
One day he ran against a knife
    In the hands of old Bob Cline—
So over Jake we held a wake,
    In the Days of 'Forty-Nine.

There was Rackensack Jim, who could outroar
    A Buffalo Bull, you bet!
He would roar all night, he would roar all day,
    And I b'lieve he's a-roaring yet!
One night he fell in a prospect-hole—
    'T was a roaring bad design—
For in that hole he roared out his soul
    In the Days of 'Forty-Nine.

There was Poor Lame Ches, a hard old case
    Who never did repent.
Ches never missed a single meal,
    Nor he never paid a cent.
But Poor Lame Ches, like all the rest,
    Did to death at last resign,
For all in his bloom he went up the Flume
    In the Days of 'Forty-Nine.

And now my comrades all are gone,
    Not one remains to toast;
They have left me here in my misery,
    Like some poor wandering ghost.
And as I go from place to place,
    Folks call me a "Travelling Sign,"
Saying "There goes Tom Moore, a Bummer, sure,
    From the Days of 'Forty-Nine."

Be courteous to all, but intimate with few, and let those few be well tried before you give them your confidence. True friendship is a plant of slow growth, and must undergo and withstand the shocks of adversity before it is entitled to the appellation.

—GEORGE WASHINGTON
(1732–1799)

We may build more splendid habitations, fill our rooms with paintings and with sculptures. But we cannot buy with gold the old associations.

—HENRY WADSWORTH
LONGFELLOW (1807–1882)

Yes'm, old friends is always best, 'less you can catch a new one that's fit to make an old one out of.

—NEW ENGLAND WRITER
SARAH ORNE JEWETT
(1849–1909)

THERE IS NO FRIEND LIKE AN OLD FRIEND

There is no friend like an old friend
Who has shared our morning days,
No greeting like his welcome,
No homage like his praise.

—OLIVER WENDELL HOLMES (1841–1935)

Friends are born, not made.

—HENRY ADAMS (1838–1918)

"Beth Finds the Palace Beautiful"

— A retelling from
Little Women, by
Louisa May Alcott

First published in 1868, Little Women *was the result of a request by Louisa May Alcott's publisher that she write "something for girls." Louisa wrote effortlessly, basing the work on her own "Pathetic Little Family," as she called the Alcotts. "Jo" represents Louisa herself; "Meg" is her older sister; "Beth," about whom this selection is written, is Lizzie; and "Amy" is May, the baby of the family.*

The Laurence house next door was like a palace to the four March sisters, although Beth found it difficult to pass through the doors. She went once with Jo, but the old gentleman, unaware of her "infirmity," as Beth called her shyness, frightened her with his gruff manner, so much so that she ran home and told her mother that she was never going back there. Still, she longed to play the beautiful piano in the drawing room.

When Mr. Laurence was informed of her shyness, he made it his business to call on the March family. The subject of music came up during their conversation, and he began to talk about the piano and the great singers who had used it for their accompaniments. Paying no special attention to any of the girls, he casually asked their mother if one of them might come over and make use of it—just to keep it in tune.

The irresistible offer filled Beth with excitement, and she had to press her hands together to keep from clapping. When Mr. Laurence added that there was no need to check in with anyone, that it was all right to merely go straight to the drawing room and play, Beth was almost overcome with joy. She slipped her little hand into his and said, "I would dearly love to come, as long as I wouldn't be a bother to anyone." Beth blushed like a rose at her boldness.

Mr. Laurence squeezed the small hand, bent down, and said, "I had a granddaughter with eyes like these." He kissed Beth's forehead and hurried away. After that, Beth's little brown hood could be seen slipping through the hedge daily as she made her way next door, where she filled the great drawing room with her tuneful spirit. She never knew that Mr. Laurence opened his study door to listen, or that the servants had been instructed to not disturb her while she played.

To show her thanks, Beth decided to make the old gentleman a pair of slippers. After much discussion with her mother about style, pattern, and cost, a deep-purple material was chosen, with cheerful pansies stitched on top. The artful girl worked daily until they were finished. She then wrote a short, simple note, and with the help of Mr. Laurence's grandson, the slippers were smuggled into his home, to be found on his study table when he arose the following morning.

Shy Beth waited to hear from Mr. Laurence, but the entire day passed, as did part of the next, with no word from him. She finally took one of her invalid dolls out for a walk. When she returned, she could see her sisters' faces peering at her excitedly from the parlor windows. Beth hurried inside and was marched directly to the parlor. There stood a small cabinet piano, delivered during her absence.

"Oh, it's too lovely," Beth cried, hiding her face while Jo read the accompanying note from Mr. Laurence aloud. He thanked her for the slippers, which he admitted were the finest he had ever worn, and in return asked her to accept the little piano, which had once belonged to his granddaughter.

Before she could lose her nerve, Beth ran next door, where she found the old gentleman sitting alone in his study. "I've come to thank you, sir, for...." But she forgot her speech, and, recalling only that he had lost a little girl very much like her, put her tiny arms around his neck and kissed him. Mr. Laurence couldn't have been more astonished, or more pleased.

Beth's fear of Mr. Laurence ceased forever that day, and they became great friends. The March sisters were delighted at Beth's newfound courage, having witnessed firsthand how love casts out fear, just as gratitude conquers pride.

Faith

aith turns the saying, "Seeing is believing" on its head; faith says, "Believing is seeing." Those who refuse to believe will never see all of what is really there. In other words, to see what lies ahead or even what lies about you, you must begin with the proper perspective. All seems lost only to those who have not first oriented themselves by the right landmarks.

Americans may not all believe in the same God or religious creed, but they have always seemed to realize that their triumphs were due in part to a force unseen by the naked eye. The American people have always seen themselves as having a special relationship with Providence, and they have derived strength and encouragement from the belief that their actions merited divine approval.

The following examples were chosen for their expressions of determination and steadfastness. Like courage, faith requires one to see the possibility of a new and better future. Beyond that, expressions of faith invite us to reflect not only upon the thoughts and actions of the faithful, but upon the object of their faith—and ultimately, to consider the question of what is worth having faith in. Simply put, faith can only be inspired by that which proves worthy of it.

Considered one of the first American poets of consequence, Anne Bradstreet (1612–1672) came to America from England in 1630, joining the Massachusetts Bay Colony. Both her husband and father served as governors of the Puritan community, whose lofty religious ideals are reflected in much of her work.

UPON THE BURNING OF OUR HOUSE
JULY 10TH, 1666

In silent night when rest I took,
For sorrow near I did not look,
I waken'd was with thundring noise
And piteous shreiks of dreadfull voice.
That fearfull sound of "Fire!" and "Fire!"
Let no man know is my Desire.

I, starting up, the light did spye,
And to my God my heart did cry
To strengthen me in my Distresse,
And not to leave me succourlesse.
Then coming out, beheld apace
The flame consume my dwelling place.

And when I could no longer look,
I blest his Name that gave and took,
That layd my goods now in the dust:
Yea so it was, and so 'twas just.
It was his own: it was not mine;
Far be it that I should repine.

He might of All justly bereft,
But yet sufficient for us left.
When by the Ruines oft I past,
My sorrowing eyes aside did cast,
And here and there the places spye
Where oft I sate, and long did lye.

Here stood that Trunk, and there that chest;
There lay that store I counted best:
My pleasant things in ashes lye,
And them behold no more shall I.
Under thy roof no guest shall sitt,
Nor at thy Table eat a bitt.

No pleasant tale shall e'er be told,
Nor things recounted done of old.
No Candle e'er shall shine in Thee,
Nor bridegroom's voice e'er heard shall bee.
In silence ever shalt thou lye;
Adeiu, Adeiu; All's vanity.

Then streight I 'gan my heart to chide:
And did thy wealth on earth abide?
Didst fix thy hope on mouldring dust,
The arm of flesh didst make thy trust?
Raise up thy thoughts above the skye,
That dunghill mists away may flie.

Thou hast an house on high erect,
Fram'd by that mighty Architect,
With glory richly furnished,
Stands permanent though this bee fled.
It's purchased, and paid for, too,
By Him who hath enough to doe.

A Prise so vast as is unknown,
Yet, by his Gift, is made thine own.
There's wealth enough, I need no more;
Farewell my Pelf, farewell my Store.
The world no longer let me Love,
My Hope and Treasure lyes Above.

A Dollar's Worth of Faith

—By Becky Bell

When Jamie was eight years old, a missionary came to her church to speak about mission work in Peru. Pastor Tom was a pilot, and he told them exciting stories about life in Peru and about the places he visited by plane. Jamie especially liked one story about Pastor Tom landing his plane during a fierce tropical storm. He was carrying medical supplies and was able to get out of the plane just before the wind picked it up, flipped it over, and carried it away.

After church, Pastor Tom played soccer with Jamie and some of her friends from Sunday School. Jamie really liked him. She even imagined what it would be like to be a missionary pilot when she grew up.

That evening, Pastor Tom came to Jamie's home for dinner. Her family listened intently to the stories about the Peruvians and their rich history. Suddenly, Jamie got very excited. She knew she just had to do something for these people.

Jamie excused herself from the table and went upstairs to her room to get a small brown envelope from under her pillow. She pulled out a crisp one dollar bill. Aunt Joyce had sent it to her for her birthday, and she had planned to spend it on chocolate. Now she had another idea. Jamie bounded down the steps and rounded the corner to the dining room, her cheeks flushed with enthusiasm.

"Pastor Tom," she announced, "I have a dollar for you." The young missionary looked puzzled. "I want you to take my dollar and use it in Peru. Then write to me some day and tell me what you did with it."

Pastor Tom smiled broadly and took the dollar. "Thank you, Jamie. I can do just that. In the meantime, I want you to pray about this dollar and where it goes and who is touched by it. Can you do that?"

"Sure I will. I'll start tonight when I say my prayers." Pastor Tom folded the dollar and put it in his pocket Bible. Then he gave Jamie a verse to remember when she prayed. It was from the book of Luke: "If you have faith the size of a grain of mustard seed, you could say to the mulberry tree, 'Uproot yourself and be planted in the sea,' and it would obey you."

"Can you pray with that kind of faith, Jamie?"

Jamie thought hard for a moment. "Yes, sir, I'll try my best."

Jamie didn't just pray that night and then forget about it. She prayed every night for Pastor Tom to do just the right thing with her dollar. After a few weeks she prayed even more because she knew Pastor Tom was back in Peru.

Early one morning, when Jamie was eating breakfast, her mom brought her a very special envelope with a strange-looking stamp on the upper right-hand corner. Jamie knew immediately that it was the letter she had been waiting for. She opened it very carefully.

Pastor Tom wrote that he had used the dollar to buy a few copies of the Gospel of John. When he flew into a small town in the mountains to speak, he gave a copy to the families who invited him into their homes. He suggested Jamie pray that Jesus would touch their hearts as they read their first words from the Bible.

Jamie was so thrilled that she didn't just pray at night anymore. Now she was praying in the morning, too. And any other time she thought about it—which was pretty often.

Weeks passed and Jamie started back to school. She had a new teacher and a new classroom. The leaves turned colors and fell to the ground, but Jamie still hadn't heard anything more from Peru.

Finally, just before Christmas, Jamie's family received a holiday card from Pastor Tom. It included a note just for her. Because of heavy rains, Pastor Tom had not revisited the town where he had taken the gospels. Finally, he was able to go last week. He found a man who had read one of the booklets and was very enthusiastic about the word of God. Jamie's heart raced as she read the letter.

The man's name was Manuel. He was 21 years old and wanted to come to the United States to go to college. He hoped to go to a school where he could learn more about the man known as Jesus.

Jamie could hardly contain herself. Dinner was very difficult to sit through, and falling asleep that night was almost impossible. She looked at the starry sky outside her bedroom window and wondered if Manuel could see the same stars at night. Jamie was beginning to feel a connection with this man who lived so far away.

Christmas came and went. Jamie was so thankful that Jesus had given her a present this year—a present named Manuel. Jamie told her friends in Sunday School about him. She told her pastor about him. And in Show-and-Tell at school she told her class about him.

In the spring, Pastor Tom wrote again. He said that Manuel had applied for admission to a Bible college in Pennsylvania. He had decided that he wanted to be a missionary to his own people. Manuel would be starting college in the fall. He promised to work very hard so that he could come back as soon as possible to help Pastor Tom.

Jamie sat on the edge of her bed with the half-read letter in her lap. This was more than she had ever imagined. It was astonishing that God had heard her prayers and answered them in such a big way. She turned back to the letter from her friend. Pastor Tom concluded by saying that Jesus had led Jamie to do His work.

"God could have used anyone to bring Manuel to Him," Pastor Tom wrote, "but he allowed you, Jamie, to know the blessing of answered prayer."

GOD MAKES A PATH

God makes a path, provides a guide,
    And feeds a wilderness;
His glorious name, while breath remains,
    O that I may confess.

Lost many a time, I have had no guide,
    No house but a hollow tree!
In stormy winter night no fire,
    No food, no company;

In Him I found a house, a bed,
    A table, company;
No cup so bitter but's made sweet,
    Where God shall sweetening be.

—CLERGYMAN AND RHODE ISLAND FOUNDER
ROGER WILLIAMS (1603–1683)

WHAT GOD HATH PROMISED

God hath not promised
Skies always blue,
Flower-strewn pathways
All our lives through;
God hath not promised
Sun without rain,
Joy without sorrow,
Peace without pain.

But God hath promised
Strength for the day,
Rest for the labor,
Light for the way,
Grace for the trials,
Help from above,
Unfailing sympathy,
Undying love.

—ANNIE JOHNSON FLINT (1862–1932)

A successful publisher and editor, James Thomas Fields (1817–1881) is the author of several books, including two volumes of poetry. "Ballad of the Tempest" is one of his best-known poems.

BALLAD OF THE TEMPEST

We were crowded in the cabin
    Not a soul would dare to sleep,—
It was midnight on the waters,
    And a storm was on the deep.

'Tis a fearful thing in winter
    To be shattered by the blast,
And to hear the rattling trumpet
    Thunder, "Cut away the mast!"

So we shuddered there in silence,—
    For the stoutest held his breath,
While the hungry sea was roaring
    And the breakers talked with death.

As thus we sat in darkness
    Each one busy with his prayers,
"We are lost!" the captain shouted,
    As he staggered down the stairs.

But his little daughter whispered,
    As she took his icy hand,
"Isn't God upon the ocean,
    Just the same as on the land?"

Then we kissed the little maiden,
    And we spake in better cheer,
And we anchored safe in harbor
    When the morn was shining clear.

General George S. Patton, Jr.'s 1947 book, War As I Knew It, *includes annotations by Colonel Paul D. Harkins, who served under the feisty commander during World War II. Harkins recalls the following account about the general's decision to seek God's help in the war effort.*

 n or about the fourteenth of December, 1944, General Patton called Chaplain O'Neill, Third Army Chaplain, and myself into his office in Third Headquarters at Nancy. The conversation went something like this:

General Patton: "Chaplain, I want you to publish a prayer for good weather. I'm tired of these soldiers having to fight mud and floods as well as Germans. See if we can't get God to work on our side."

Chaplain O'Neill: "Sir, it's going to take a pretty thick rug for that kind of praying."

General Patton: "I don't care if it takes the flying carpet. I want the praying done."

Chaplain O'Neill: "Yes, sir. May I say, General, that it usually isn't a customary thing among men of my profession to pray for clear weather to kill fellow men."

General Patton: "Chaplain, are you teaching me theology or are you the Chaplain of the Third Army? I want a prayer."

Chaplain O'Neill: "Yes, sir."

Outside, the Chaplain said, "Whew, that's a tough one! What do you think he wants?"

It was perfectly clear to me. The General wanted a prayer—he wanted one right now—and he wanted it published to the Command.

The Army Engineer was called in, and we finally decided that our field topographical company could print the prayer on a small-sized card, making enough copies for distribution to the army.

It being near Christmas, we also decided to ask General Patton to include a Christmas greeting to the troops on the same card with the prayer. The General agreed, wrote a short greeting, and the card was made up, published, and distributed to the troops on the twenty-second of December.

"Chaplain, I want you to publish a prayer for good weather," the general ordered. "See if we can't get God to work on our side."

Actually, the prayer was offered in order to bring clear weather for the planned Third Army break-through to the Rhine in the Saarguemines area, then scheduled for December 21.

The Bulge put a crimp in these plans. As it happened, the Third Army had moved north to attack the south flank of the Bulge when the prayer was actually issued.

PRAYER

Almighty and most merciful Father, we humbly beseech Thee, of Thy great goodness, to restrain these immoderate rains with which we have had to contend. Grant us fair weather for Battle. Graciously hearken to us as soldiers who call upon Thee that, armed with Thy power, we may advance from victory to victory, and crush the oppression and wickedness of our enemies, and establish Thy justice among men and nations. Amen.

(REVERSE SIDE)

To each officer and soldier in the Third United States Army, I wish a Merry Christmas. I have full confidence in your courage, devotion to duty, and skill in battle. We march in our might to complete victory. May God's blessing rest upon each of you on this Christmas Day.

G. S. PATTON, JR.
Lieutenant General
Commanding, Third United States Army

Whether it was the help of the Divine guidance asked for in the prayer or just the normal course of human events, we never knew; at any rate, on the twenty-third, the day after the prayer was issued, the weather cleared and remained perfect for about six days. Enough to allow the Allies to break the backbone of the Von Rundstedt offensive and turn a temporary setback into a crushing defeat for the enemy.

We had moved our advanced Headquarters to Luxembourg at this time to be closer to the battle area. The bulk of the Army Staff, including the Chaplain, was still in Nancy. General Patton again called me to his office. He wore a smile from ear to ear. He said, "God damn! look at the weather. That O'Neill sure did some potent praying. Get him up here. I want to pin a medal on him."

The Chaplain came up next day. The weather was still clear when we walked into General Patton's office. The General rose, came from behind his desk with hand outstretched and said, "Chaplain, you're the most popular man in this Headquarters. You sure stand in good with the Lord and soldiers." The General then pinned a Bronze Star Medal on Chaplain O'Neill.

Everyone offered congratulations and thanks and we got back to the business of killing Germans—with clear weather for battle.

UNBELIEF

There is no unbelief;
Whoever plants a seed beneath the sod
And waits to see it push away the clod,
    He trusts in God.

Whoever says when clouds are in the sky,
"Be patient, heart; light breaketh by and by,"
    Trusts the Most High.

Whoever sees 'neath winter's field of snow,
The silent harvest of the future grow,
    God's power must know.

Whoever lies down on his couch to sleep,
Content to lock each sense in slumber deep,
    Knows God will keep.

Whoever says "To-morrow," "The unknown,"
"The future," trusts that Power alone
    He dares disown.

The heart that looks on when the eye-lids close,
And dares to live when life has only woes,
    God's comfort knows.

    There is no unbelief;
For thus by day and night unconsciously
The heart lives by the faith the lips deny.
    God knoweth why!

—ELIZABETH YORK CASE (1840–1911)

SCHOOL DAYS

Lord, let me make this rule:
To think of life as school,
    And try my best
    To stand each test,
    And do my work
    And nothing shirk.

If weary with my book
I cast a wistful look
    Where posies grow,
    Oh, let me know
    That flowers within
    Are best to win.

These lessons thou dost give
To teach me how to live,
    To do, to bear,
    To get and share,
    To work and play
    And trust alway.

Some day the bell will sound,
Some day my heart will bound,
    As with a shout,
    That school is out,
    And, lessons done,
    I homeward run.

—MALTBIE D. BABCOCK (1858–1901)

In God We Trust.

—LONGTIME MOTTO OF THE
UNITED STATES; IMPRINTED
ON U.S. CURRENCY SINCE 1864

I never saw a Moor—
I never saw the Sea—
Yet know I how the Heather looks
And what a Billow be.

I never spoke with God
Nor visited in Heaven—
Yet certain am I of the spot
As if the Checks were given—

—EMILY DICKINSON (1830–1886)

t is only when the apparent absurdity of life is faced in all truth that faith really becomes possible. Otherwise, faith tends to be a kind of diversion, a spiritual amusement, in which one gathers up accepted, conventional formulas and arranges them in the approved mental patterns, without bothering to investigate their meaning, or asking if they have any practical consequences in one's life.

—CLERGYMAN AND WRITER
THOMAS MERTON
(1915–1968)

ll human action, all good endeavor, all the progress of civilization, is the work of faith....

Thus we see that faith abides,—faith in truths as yet unseen, in laws not yet discovered, in great realities outside of our present vision. All human knowledge, human endeavor, earthly progress depends on faith that beyond what we know there is a great world of truth and good still to be discovered.

And this is, in reality, faith in God. For God is the eternal Truth, the omniscient Good. He is behind all things, before all things, and above all things. We do not see him, but faith leads directly and inevitably to him.

—CLERGYMAN JAMES FREEMAN CLARKE (1810–1888)

Neither party expected for the war, the magnitude, or the duration, which it has already attained. Neither anticipated that the *cause* of the conflict might cease with, or even before, the conflict itself should cease.

Each looked for an easier triumph, and a result less fundamental and astounding. Both read the same Bible, and pray to the same God; and each invokes His aid against the other. It may seem strange that any men should dare to ask a just God's assistance in wringing their bread from the sweat of other men's faces; but let us judge not that we be not judged. The prayers of both could not be answered; that of neither has been answered fully. The Almighty has His own purposes. "Woe unto the world because of offences! for it must needs be that offences come; but woe to that man by whom the offence cometh!"

"Fondly do we hope— fervently do we pray—that this scourge of war may speedily pass away."

If we shall suppose that American Slavery is one of those offences which, in the providence of God, must needs come, but which, having continued through His appointed time, He now wills to remove, and that He gives to both North and South, this terrible war, as the woe due to those by whom the offence came, shall we discern therein any departure from those divine attributes which the believers in a Living God always ascribe to Him?

Fondly do we hope—fervently do we pray—that this mighty scourge of war may speedily pass away. Yet, if God wills that it continue, until all the wealth piled by the bond-man's two hundred and fifty years of unrequited toil shall be sunk, and until every drop of blood drawn with the lash, shall be paid by another drawn with the sword, as was said three thousand years ago, so still it must be said "the judgments of the Lord, are true and righteous altogether."

With malice toward none; with charity for all; with firmness in the right, as God gives us to see the right, let us strive on to finish the work we are in; to bind up the nation's wounds; to care for him who shall have borne the battle, and for his widow, and his orphan—to do all which may achieve and cherish a just, and a lasting peace, among ourselves, and with all nations.

—ABRAHAM LINCOLN, FROM HIS SECOND INAUGURAL ADDRESS, MARCH 4, 1865

A Hymn

Lead gently, Lord, and slow,
    For oh, my steps are weak,
And ever as I go,
    Some soothing sentence speak;

That I may turn my face
    Through doubt's obscurity
Toward thine abiding-place,
    E'en tho' I cannot see.

For lo, the way is dark;
    Through mist and cloud I grope,
Save for that fitful spark,
    The little flame of hope.

Lead gently, Lord, and slow,
    For fear that I may fall;
I know not where to go
    Unless I hear thy call.

My fainting soul doth yearn
    For thy green hills afar;
So let thy mercy burn —
    My greater, guiding star!

        —Paul Laurence Dunbar
        (1872–1906)

Two Prayers

Last night my little boy confessed to me
Some childish wrong;
And kneeling at my knee,
He prayed with tears —
"Dear God, make me a man
Like Daddy — wise and strong;
I know you can."

Then while he slept
I knelt beside his bed,
Confessed my sins,
And prayed with low-bowed head.
"O God, make me a child
Like my child here —
Pure, guileless,
Trusting Thee with faith sincere."

        —Andrew Gillies (1870–1942)

How plain it is, in all the most forward demonstrations of the race, that man is a creature for religion; a creature secretly allied to God himself, as the needle is to the pole, attracted toward God, aspiring consciously, or unconsciously, to the friendship and love of God....

The way of peace we cannot know, till we find our peace, where our immortal aspirations place it, in the fullness and the friendly eternity of God.

—CLERGYMAN AND WRITER HORACE BUSHNELL (1802–1876), FROM HIS "DISCOURSE ON THE DIGNITY OF HUMAN NATURE SHOWN FROM ITS RUINS"

The child lives in a world which imagination creates, where faith, hope, and love beckon to realms of beauty and delight. The spiritual and moral truths which are to become the very life-breath of his soul he apprehends mystically, not logically. Heaven lies about him; he lives in wonderland and feels the thrill of awe as naturally as he looks with wide-open eyes. Do not seek to persuade him by telling him that honesty is the best policy, that poverty overtakes the drunkard, that lechery breeds disease, that to act for the common welfare is the surest way to get what is good for oneself; for such teaching will not only leave him unimpressed, but it will seem to him profane and almost immoral. He wants to feel that he is the child of God, of the infinitely good and all-wonderful; that in his father, divine wisdom and strength are revealed; in his mother, divine tenderness and love. He so believes and trusts in God that it is our fault if he knows that men can be base.

—JOHN L. SPALDING, FORMER ROMAN CATHOLIC BISHOP OF PEORIA, ILLINOIS, FROM HIS BOOK *MEANS AND ENDS OF EDUCATION* (1903)

FAITH

O World, thou choosest not the
    better part!
It is not wisdom to be only wise,
And on the inward vision
    close the eyes,
But it is wisdom to believe the
    heart.
Columbus found a world, and
    had no chart,
Save one that faith deciphered
    in the skies;
To trust the soul's invincible
    surmise
Was all his science and his
    only art.
Our knowledge is a torch of
    smoky pine
That lights the pathway but
    one step ahead
Across a void of mystery and
    dread.
Bid, then, the tender light of
    faith to shine
By which alone the mortal heart
    is led
Unto the thinking of the
    thought divine.

—POET AND PHILOSOPHER GEORGE
    SANTAYANA (1863–1952)

Our fathers fled from the rage of prelatical tyranny and persecution, and came into this land in order to enjoy liberty of conscience, and they have increased to a great people. Many have been the interpositions of Divine Providence on our behalf, both in our fathers' days and ours; and, though we are now engaged in a war with Great Britain, yet we have been prospered in a most wonderful manner. And can we think that he who has thus far helped us will give us up into the hands of our enemies? Certainly he that has begun to deliver us will continue to show his mercy towards us, in saving us from the hands of our enemies: he will not forsake us if we do not forsake him. Our cause is so just and good that nothing can prevent our success but only our sins. Could I see a spirit of repentance and reformation prevail through the land, I should not have the least apprehension or fear of being brought under the iron rod of slavery, even though all the powers of the globe were combined against us. And

though I confess that the irreligion and profaneness which are so common among us gives something of a damp to my spirits, yet I cannot help hoping, and even believing, that Providence has designed this continent for to be the asylum of liberty and true religion; for can we suppose that the God who created us free agents, and designed that we should glorify and serve him in this world that we might enjoy him forever hereafter, will suffer liberty and true religion to be banished from off the face of the earth? But do we not find that both religion and liberty seem to be expiring and gasping for life in the other continent?— where, then, can they find a harbor or place of refuge but in this?

—SAMUEL WEST, PASTOR OF A CHURCH IN DARTMOUTH, FROM "THE ELECTION
    SERMON," DELIVERED IN BOSTON ON MAY 29, 1776

Samuel Morse invented the telegraph during the 1830s while he was a professor at the University of the City of New York. Although he felt confident about his eventual success, it took several difficult years to fully develop and promote his then-revolutionary invention. Following is an excerpt from a letter to his brother Sidney dated January 20, 1843.

y patience is still tried in waiting for the action of Congress on my bill. With so much at stake you may easily conceive how tantalizing is this state of suspense.... At times, after waiting all day and day after day, in the hope that my bill may be called up, and in vain, I feel heartsick, and finding nothing accomplished, that no progress is made, that precious time flies, I am depressed and begin to question whether I am in the way of duty. But when I feel that I have done all in my power, and that this delay may be designed by the wise Disposer of all events for a trial of patience, I find relief and a disposition quietly to wait such issue as He shall direct, knowing that, if I sincerely have put my trust in Him, He will not lead me astray, and my way will, in any event, be made plain.

i thank You God for most this amazing

A literary nonconformist, Edward Estlin Cummings (1894–1962)—better known as e. e. cummings (he had his name changed legally to lowercase letters only)—was a poet and painter who was known for his eccentric punctuation and spelling. Cummings' moods were alternately satirical and tough or, as in the following work, tender and childlike.

i thank You God for most this amazing
day:for the leaping greenly spirits of trees
and a blue true dream of sky;and for everything
which is natural which is infinite which is yes

(i who have died am alive again today,
and this is the sun's birthday;this is the birth
day of life and of love and wings:and of the gay
great happening illimitably earth)

how should tasting touching hearing seeing
breathing any—lifted from the no
of all nothing—human merely being
doubt unimaginable You?

(now the ears of my ears awake and
now the eyes of my eyes are opened)

Faith enables our spiritual sense to function.

—A. W. TOZER

THE HIGHER GOOD

Father, I will not ask for wealth or fame,
    Though once they would have joyed my carnal sense:
I shudder not to bear a hated name,
    Wanting all wealth, myself my sole defence.
But give me, Lord, eyes to behold the truth;
    A seeing sense that knows the eternal right;
A heart with pity filled, and gentlest ruth;
    A manly faith that makes all darkness light:
Give me the power to labor for mankind;
    Make me the mouth of such as cannot speak;
Eyes let me be to groping men, and blind;
    A conscience to the base; and to the weak
Let me be hands and feet; and to the foolish, mind;
And lead still further on such as thy kingdom seek.

—CLERGYMAN THEODORE PARKER (1810–1860)

STILL, STILL WITH THEE

Still, still with Thee, when purple morning breaketh,
　　When the bird waketh and the shadows flee,
Fairer than morning, lovelier than the daylight,
　　Dawns the sweet consciousness, I am with Thee!

Alone with Thee, amid the mystic shadows,
　　The solemn hush of nature newly born;
Alone with Thee, in breathless adoration,
　　In the calm dew and freshness of the morn.

Still, still with Thee, as to each new-born morning
　　A fresh and solemn splendor still is given,
So doth this blessed consciousness awakening,
　　Breathe, each day, nearness unto Thee and heaven.

When sinks the soul, subdued by toil, to slumber,
　　Its closing eye looks up to Thee in prayer;
Sweet the repose beneath Thy wings o'ershading,
　　But sweeter still to wake and find Thee there.

So shall it be at last, in that bright morning
　　When the soul waketh and life's shadows flee;
Oh, in that hour fairer than daylight dawning,
　　Shall rise the glorious thought, I am with Thee!

—AUTHOR HARRIET BEECHER STOWE (1811–1896)

Humor

Although humor is routinely employed as a defense mechanism, particularly on an individual level, for Americans as a group it has also proven to be a very useful weapon. "Irreverence is the champion of liberty," insisted humorist Mark Twain, "and its only sure defense." For once in his life, he was serious.

Surely nothing punctures pretentiousness—our own or someone else's—like a bit of well-aimed wit, and few people knew this better than Will Rogers. "My forefathers didn't come over on the *Mayflower*," the actor and humorist, who proudly claimed to be part Indian, once told an audience, "but they met the boat."

Some of the most revered Americans have been people who had a gift for making others laugh—and who could just as easily laugh at themselves. Abraham Lincoln, for example, was well-known for telling funny stories about himself. His self-effacing nature was one of the qualities that endeared him to millions of his countrymen.

The best humor, someone once said, involves common perceptions being suddenly overturned. True or not, Americans have revealed a special talent for seeing the world in fresh, new ways.

THE WORST WAY

Lincoln attended his first ball in Springfield (Illinois) because he wished to see Mary Todd. "Miss Todd," he said, "I should like to dance with you the worst way." Afterward Mary told a friend: "He certainly did!"

—FROM *PRESIDENTIAL ANECDOTES*, BY PAUL F. BOLLER, JR. (1981, OXFORD UNIVERSITY PRESS)

Humor is wit with a rooster's tail feathers stuck in its cap.

—AMERICAN PROVERB

Good humor is the suspenders that keep our working clothes on.

—AMERICAN PROVERB

If congressmen talk too much, how can it be otherwise in a body to which the people send one hundred and fifty lawyers, whose trade it is to question everything, yield nothing, and talk by the hour?

—THOMAS JEFFERSON, 1821

Work consists of whatever a body is obliged to do....
Play consists of whatever a body is not obliged to do.

—MARK TWAIN, FROM *THE ADVENTURES OF TOM SAWYER* (1876)

WILL ROGERS MEETS CAL

Just before Will Rogers first met President Coolidge, one of his friends said, "I'll bet you can't make Cal laugh in two minutes." "I'll bet he laughs in 20 seconds," said Will. Then came the introduction: "Mr. President, this is Mr. Will Rogers; Mr. Rogers, President Coolidge." Will held out his hand, looked confused, then said, "Excuse me, I didn't quite get the name." And a grin spread over Coolidge's face.

—FROM *PRESIDENTIAL ANECDOTES*, BY
PAUL F. BOLLER, JR. (1981,
OXFORD UNIVERSITY PRESS)

HUCK FINN DISCOVERS MOSES

Considered by many scholars to be Mark Twain's finest book, The Adventures of Huckleberry Finn *(1884), from which the following excerpt is taken, is narrated by its title character, the uneducated son of a village drunkard. Huckleberry's use of vernacular speech, coupled with his uninhibited youthfulness and general lack of sophistication, creates a narrative that is comical yet subtly ironic.*

The Widow Douglas she took me for her son, and allowed she would sivilize me; but it was rough living in the house all the time, considering how dismal regular and decent the widow was in all her ways; and so when I couldn't stand it no longer I lit out. I got into my old rags and my sugar hogshead again, and was free and satisfied. But Tom Sawyer he hunted me up and said he was going to start a band of robbers, and I might join if I would go back to the widow and be respectable. So I went back.

The widow she cried over me, and called me a poor lost lamb, and she called me a lot of other names, too, but she never meant no harm by it. She put me in them new clothes again, and I couldn't do nothing but sweat and sweat, and feel all cramped up. Well, then, the old thing commenced again. The widow rung a bell for supper, and you had to come to time. When you got to the table you couldn't go right to eating, but you had to wait for the widow to tuck down her head and grumble a little over the victuals, though there warn't really anything the matter with them. . . .

After supper she got out her book and learned me about Moses and the Bulrushers, and I was in a sweat to find out all about him; but by and by she let it out that Moses had been dead a considerable long time; so then I didn't care no more about him, because I don't take no stock in dead people.

Pretty soon I wanted to smoke, and asked the widow to let me. But she wouldn't. She said it was a mean practice and wasn't clean, and I must try to not do it any more. That is just the way with some people. They get down on a thing when they don't know nothing about it. Here she was a-bothering about Moses, which was no kin to her, and no use to anybody, being gone, you see, yet finding a power of fault with me for doing a thing that had some good in it. And she took snuff, too; of course that was all right, because she done it herself.

Her sister, Miss Watson, a tolerable slim old maid, with goggles on, had just come to live with her, and took a set at me now with a spelling book. She worked me middling hard for about an hour, and then the widow made her ease up. I couldn't stood it much longer. Then for an hour it was deadly dull, and I was fidgety. Miss Watson would say, "Don't put your feet up there, Huckleberry"; and "Don't scrunch up like that, Huckleberry—set up straight"; and pretty soon she would say, "Don't gap and stretch like that, Huckleberry—why don't you try to behave?" Then she told me all about the bad place, and I said I wished I was there. She got mad then, but I didn't mean no harm. All I wanted was to go somewheres; all I wanted was a change, I warn't particular. She said it was wicked to say what I said; said she wouldn't say it for the whole world; *she* was going to live so as to go to the good place. Well, I couldn't see no advantage in going where she was going, so I made up my mind I wouldn't try for it. But I never said so, because it would only make trouble, and wouldn't do no good.

Now she had got a start, and she went on and told me all about the good place. She said all a body would have to do there was to go around all day long with a harp and sing, forever and ever. So I didn't think much of it. But I never said so. I asked her if she reckoned Tom Sawyer would go there, and she said not by a considerable sight. I was glad about that, because I wanted him and me to be together.

THE LAST TRAIN

A year or two after he became President, John Tyler decided to take a trip and sent his son Bob to order a special train. The railroad superintendent, a devout Whig, told Bob that he didn't run special trains for Presidents. "What!" cried Bob. "Didn't you furnish a special train for the funeral of General Harrison?" "Yes," said the superintendent. "And if you will bring your father here in that shape, you shall have the best train on the road!"

—FROM *PRESIDENTIAL ANECDOTES*, BY
    PAUL F. BOLLER, JR. (1981,
    OXFORD UNIVERSITY PRESS)

In response to a child's letter requesting his autograph, President Herbert Hoover wrote back:

I was delighted to see that you were not a professional autograph hunter. Once upon a time, one of those asked me for three autographs. I inquired why. He said, "It takes two of yours to get one of Babe Ruth's."

—FROM *PRESIDENTIAL WIT*, BY BILL ADLER (1966, TRIDENT PRESS)

During a campaign speech, Theodore Roosevelt found himself being constantly interrupted by a drunk who kept shouting, "I'm a Democrat."

Roosevelt stopped his speech, turned to the man and said, "May I ask the gentleman why he is a Democrat?"

The drunk replied, "My grandfather was a Democrat; my father was a Democrat; and I am a Democrat."

Roosevelt then asked, "My friend, suppose your grandfather had been a jackass and your father had been a jackass, what would you be?" and the drunk replied instantly, "A Republican!"

—From *Presidential Wit*, by Bill Adler (1966, Trident Press)

A frontiersman lost his way in an uninhabited region on a dark and tempestuous night. The rain fell in torrents, accompanied by terrible thunder and more terrific lightning. His trouble increased when his horse halted, being exhausted with fatigue and fright. Presently a bolt of lightning struck a neighboring tree, and the crash brought the man to his knees. He was not an expert in prayer, but his appeal was short and to the point: "O Lord, if it is all the same to you, give us a little more light, and a little less noise!"

—"Lincoln Humor Sampler" from *Lincoln, an Illustrated Biography* (1993, Knopf)

THE WEATHER IN NEW ENGLAND

An excerpt from a lecture presented by humorist Mark Twain at the annual dinner of the New England Society on December 22, 1876.

I reverently believe that the Maker who made us all, makes everything in New England—but the weather. I don't know who makes that, but I think it must be raw apprentices in the Weather Clerk's factory, who experiment and learn how in New England for board and clothes, and then are promoted to make weather for countries that require a good article and will take their custom elsewhere if they don't get it. There is a sumptuous variety about the New England weather that compels the stranger's admiration—and regret. The weather is always doing something there; always attending strictly to business; always getting up new designs and trying them on the people to see how they will go. But it gets through more business in spring than in any other season. In the spring I have counted one hundred and thirty-six different kinds of weather inside of four and twenty hours. . . .

> *"New England can't hold a tenth of her weather. You can see cracks all about, where she has strained herself trying to do it."*

Yes, one of the brightest gems in the New England weather is the dazzling uncertainty of it. There is only one thing certain about it, you are certain there is going to be plenty of weather, a perfect grand review; but you never can tell which end of the procession is going to move first. You fix up for the drought; you leave your umbrella in the house and sally out with your sprinkling-pot, and ten to one you get drowned. You make up your mind that the earthquake is due; you stand from under and take hold of something to steady yourself, and the first thing you know, you get struck by lightning. . . .

Now, as to the size of the weather in New England—lengthways, I mean. It is utterly disproportioned to the size of that little country. Half the time, when it is packed as full as it can stick, you will see that New England weather sticking out beyond the edges and projecting around hundreds and hundreds of miles over the neighboring States. She can't hold a tenth part of her weather. You can see cracks all about, where she has strained herself trying to do it.

A temperance advocate visited Lincoln at the White House to protest the whiskey-drinking of General Grant. After listening to the complaint, Lincoln said:

"Find out the brand of whiskey General Grant uses. I would like to furnish the same brand to my other generals."

—From *Presidential Wit,* by Bill Adler (1966, Trident Press)

To see some people you would think that the essential of orthodox Christianity is to have a face so long you could eat oatmeal out of the end of a gas pipe. Sister, that is not religion; I want to tell you that the smiling, happy, sunny-faced religion will win more people to Jesus Christ than the miserable old, grim-faced kind will in 10 years.

I pity anyone who can't laugh. There must be something wrong with their religion or their lives. The devil can't laugh.

—William A. (Billy) Sunday (1862–1935), former baseball star turned preacher, from one of his often-repeated revival sermons

You cannot live without the lawyers, and certainly you cannot die without them.

—Lawyer and diplomat Joseph Hodges Choate (1832–1917)

THE HOSS

Sometimes called "the poet of the people," Indiana native James Whitcomb Riley (1849–1916) gained a reputation for his nostalgic dialect verse. Here he pays tribute to the horse.

The hoss he is a splendud beast;
     He is man's friend, as heaven desined,
And, search the world from west to east,
     No honester you'll ever find!

Some calls the hoss "a pore dumb brute,"
     And yit, like Him who died fer you,
I say, as I theyr charge refute,
     "'Fergive; they know not what they do!'"

No wiser animal makes tracks
     Upon these earthly shores, and hence
Arose the axium, true as facts,
     Extoled by all, as "Good hoss-sense!"

The hoss is strong, and knows his stren'th,
     You hitch him up a time er two
And lash him, and he'll go his len'th
     And kick the dashboard out fer you!

But, treat him allus good and kind,
     And never strike him with a stick,
Ner aggervate him, and you'll find
     He'll never do a hostile trick.

A hoss whose master tends him right
     And worters him with daily care,
Will do your biddin' with delight,
     And act as docile as *you* air.

He'll paw and prance to hear your praise,
    Because he's learnt to love you well;
And, though you can't tell what he says,
    He'll nicker all he wants to tell.

He knows you when you slam the gate
    At early dawn, upon your way
Unto the barn, and snorts elate,
    To git his corn, er oats, er hay.

He knows you, as the orphant knows
    The folks that loves her like theyr own,
And raises her and "finds" her clothes,
    And "schools" her tel a womern-grown!

I claim no hoss will harm a man,
    Ner kick, ner run away, cavort,
Stump-suck, er balk, er "catamaran,"
    Ef you'll jest treat him as you ort.

But when I see the beast abused,
    And clubbed around as I've saw some,
I want to see his owner noosed,
    And jest yanked up like Absolum!

Of course they's differunce in stock,
    A hoss that has a little yeer,
And slender build, and shaller hock,
    Can beat his shadder, mighty near!

Whilse one that's thick in neck and chist
    And big in leg and full in flank,
That tries to race, I still insist
    He'll have to take the second rank.

And I have jest laid back and laughed,
    And rolled and wallered in the grass
At fairs, to see some heavy-draft
    Lead out at *first,* yit come in *last!*

Each hoss has his appinted place,
    The heavy hoss should plow the soil;
The blooded racer, he must race,
    And win big wages fer his toil.

I never bet — ner never wrought
    Upon my feller man to bet —
And yit, at times, I've often thought
    Of my convictions with regret.

I bless the hoss from hoof to head —
    From head to hoof, and tale to mane!
I bless the hoss, as I have said,
    From head to hoof, and back again!

I love my God the first of all,
    Then Him that perished on the cross,
And next, my wife, and then I fall
    Down on my knees and love the hoss.

GOOD WISHES FOR THANKSGIVING DAY.

WHEN FATHER CARVES THE DUCK

We all look on with anxious eyes
  When father carves the duck,
And mother almost always sighs
  When father carves the duck;
Then all of us prepare to rise,
And hold our bibs before our eyes,
And be prepared for some surprise,
  When father carves the duck.

He braces up and grabs a fork
  Whene'er he carves a duck,
And won't allow a soul to talk
  Until he's carved the duck.
The fork is jabbed into the sides,
Across the breast the knife he slides,
While every careful person hides
  From flying chips of duck.

The platter's always sure to slip
  When father carves a duck,
And how it makes the dishes skip!
  Potatoes fly amuck!
The squash and cabbage leap in space,
We get some gravy in our face,
And father mutters Hindoo grace
  Whene'er he carves a duck.

We then have learned to walk around
  The dining-room and pluck
From off the window-sills and walls
  Our share of father's duck.
While father growls and blows and jaws
And swears the knife was full of flaws,
And mother laughs at him because
  He couldn't carve a duck.

—E. V. WRIGHT

I WAVE GOOD-BYE
WHEN BUTTER FLIES

I wave good-bye when butter flies
and cheer a boxing match.
I've often watched my pillow fight,
I've sewn a cabbage patch,
I like to dance at basket balls
or lead a rubber band,
I've marveled at a spelling bee,
I've helped a peanut stand.

It's possible a pencil points,
but does a lemon drop?
Does coffee break or chocolate kiss,
and will a soda pop?
I share my milk with drinking straws,
my meals with chewing gum,
and should I see my pocket change,
I'll hear my kettle drum.

It makes me sad when lettuce leaves,
I laugh when dinner rolls,
I wonder if the kitchen sinks
and if a salad bowls,
I've listened to a diamond ring,
I've waved a football fan,
and if a chimney sweeps the floor,
I'm sure the garbage can.

—JACK PRELUTSKY, FROM *SOMETHING BIG HAS
BEEN HERE* (1990, GREENWILLOW BOOKS)

As the following account (from Presidential Wit, *by Bill Adler) demonstrates, Abraham Lincoln was not averse to joking about himself.*

One day when I first came here, I got into a fit of musing in my room and stood resting my elbows on the bureau. Looking into the glass, it struck me what an ugly man I was. The fact grew on me and I made up my mind that I must be the ugliest man in the world. It so maddened me that I resolved, should I ever see an uglier, I would shoot him on sight. Not long after this, Andy (naming a lawyer present) came to town and the first time I saw him I said to myself: "There's the man." I went home, took down my gun, and prowled around the streets waiting for him. He soon came along. "Halt, Andy," said I, pointing the gun at him; "Say your prayers, for I am going to shoot you." "Why, Mr. Lincoln, what's the matter? What have I done?" "Well, I made an oath that if I ever saw an uglier man than I am, I'd shoot him on the spot. You are uglier, surely; so make ready to die." "Mr. Lincoln, do you really think that I am uglier than you?" "Yes." "Well, Mr. Lincoln," said Andy deliberately and looking me squarely in the face, "if I am any uglier, fire away."

My forefathers didn't come over on the Mayflower, *but they met the boat.*

—Humorist Will Rogers (1879–1935), commenting on his Native American ancestry

The wife of Willis Anderson came again to petition for his pardon. She hinted that her husband did not wish to be discharged from prison himself, and that it would be no relaxation of his punishment to turn him over to her.

—John Quincy Adams, from an entry in his diary on June 19, 1828

Center Shot

Cowan and Hoffman, Western hunters, were dead shots and each hotly jealous of the other's prowess. Setting out together one day after deer, they separated in the woods, taking opposite sides of a ridge.

Almost immediately, Hoffman heard Cowan's rifle fired off. He ran over to the spot, expecting to be obliged to help hang a deer. He found Cowan reloading but no deer carcass in sight. However, a startled calf was crashing off through the hazelnut bushes.

"Oh Lord!" Hoffman whooped with delight. "You didn't shoot at that calf, did you, hoss?"

"Suppose I did?" growled Cowan.

"Why'd you do a thing like that?"

"Took it for a deer."

"Don't look like you hit it."

"No—missed."

"How in the nation did that happen?"

"Wasn't just sure that it wasn't a calf."

"That," crowed Hoffman, "is what I call a pretty sorry hunter—to shoot at a calf for a deer, and miss it at that!"

"Don't be a fool," drawled Cowan, ramming home the charge in his rifle. "I shot at it just so as to hit it if it was a deer, and miss it if it was a calf."

—Anonymous, from *The Family Book of Humor* (1957, Hanover House)

Irreverence is the champion of liberty and its only sure defense.

—MARK TWAIN (1835–1910)

WHAT LACK WE YET?

When Washington was president
    He was a mortal icicle;
He never on a railroad went,
    And never rode a bicycle.

He read by no electric lamp,
    Ne'er heard about the Yellowstone;
He never licked a postage stamp,
    And never saw a telephone.

His trousers ended at his knees;
    By wire he could not snatch dispatch;
He filled his lamp with whale-oil grease,
    And never had a match to scratch.

But in these days it's come to pass,
    All work is with such dashing done,
We've all these things, but then, alas—
    We seem to have no Washington!

—ROBERT J. BURDETTE (1844–1914)

We must learn by laughter, as well as by tears and terrors; explore the whole of nature, the farce and buffoonery in the yard below, as well as the lessons of poets and philosophers upstairs in the hall, and get the rest and refreshment of the shaking of the sides.

—RALPH WALDO EMERSON, FROM *THE COMIC* (1883)

BALLAD OF A BONELESS CHICKEN

I'm a basic boneless chicken,
yes, I have no bones inside,
I'm without a trace of rib cage,
yet I hold myself with pride.
Other hens appear offended
by my total lack of bones,
they discuss me impolitely
in derogatory tones.

I am absolutely boneless,
I am boneless through and through,
I have neither neck nor thighbones,
and my back is boneless too,
and I haven't got a wishbone,
not a bone within my breast,
so I rarely care to travel
from the comfort of my nest.

I have feathers fine and fluffy,
I have lovely little wings,
but I lack the superstructure
to support these splendid things.
Since a chicken finds it tricky
to parade on boneless legs,
I stick closely to to the hen house,
laying little scrambled eggs.

—JACK PRELUTSKY, FROM *THE NEW KID ON THE BLOCK* (1984, GREENWILLOW BOOKS)

Perseverance

After settling a continent, establishing a democratic republic without equal, and subsequently building the wealthiest industrial nation on earth—this while surviving a civil war, the Great Depression, countless natural and manmade disasters, and a couple of World Wars thrown in for good measure—Americans can claim to know a little something about the virtue of perseverance.

We all know there is no substitute for hard work. "Perseverance will accomplish all things," says the familiar old proverb. Put another way, hard work is what gives a dream legs and makes it walk.

"I learned this:" said Henry David Thoreau of his time spent in Walden Woods, "that if one advances confidently in the direction of his dreams, and endeavors to live the life which he had imagined, he will meet with a success unexpected in common hours."

Perseverance is somewhat of a homely virtue—none too flashy as virtues go—but something deep within us makes us respect the person who refuses to quit and who gets the job done. Nineteenth-century humorist Josh Billings got it right when he cracked, "Consider the postage stamp: Its usefulness consists in the ability to stick to one thing till it gets there."

"What's to become of us, Ma?"
"Can't nobody wipe us out. We'll go on forever, 'cause we're the people."

—Exchange between Ma Joad and her husband in the final scene of the 1940 film version of John Steinbeck's *The Grapes of Wrath.*

I know of no more encouraging fact than the unquestionable ability of man to elevate his life by a conscious endeavor.

—Henry David Thoreau (1817–1862)

We dare not forget today that we are the heirs of that first revolution. Let the word go forth from this time and place, to friend and foe alike, that the torch has been passed to a new generation of Americans—born in this century, tempered by war, disciplined by a hard and bitter peace, proud of our ancient heritage—and unwilling to witness or permit the slow undoing of those human rights to which this Nation has always been committed, and to which we are committed today at home and around the world.

Let every nation know, whether it wishes us well or ill, that we shall pay any price, bear any burden, meet any hardship, support any friend, oppose any foe, in order to assure the survival and the success of liberty.

This much we pledge—and more.

—John F. Kennedy, from his Inaugural Address on January 20, 1961

Consider the postage stamp:
Its usefulness consists in the
ability to stick to one thing
till it gets there.

—HUMORIST HENRY WHEELER
SHAW (1818–1885), WHO
WROTE UNDER THE PEN
NAME JOSH BILLINGS

If we had no winter, the spring would not be so pleasant; if we did not sometimes taste of adversity, prosperity would not be so welcome.

—ANNE BRADSTREET (1612–1672),
FROM *THE AMERICAN PURITANS:
THEIR PROSE AND POETRY*
(ANCHOR BOOKS, 1956)

Nothing in the world can take the place of persistence. Talent will not; nothing is more common than unsuccessful men of talent. Genius will not; unrewarded genius is almost a proverb. Education will not; the world is full of educated derelicts. Persistence and determination alone are omnipotent.

—CALVIN COOLIDGE (1872–1933)

DON'T QUIT

When things go wrong, as they sometimes will,
 When the road you're trudging seems all up hill,
. . . When care is pressing you down a bit,
Rest, if you must—but don't you quit.
. . . Often the goal is nearer than
It seems to a faint and faltering man,
Often the struggler has given up
When he might have captured the victor's cup.

—AUTHOR UNKNOWN; FROM *THE BEST LOVED POEMS OF
THE AMERICAN PEOPLE* (HAZEL FELLEMAN, 1936)

Diligence is the Mother of Good luck.

—BENJAMIN FRANKLIN
(1706–1790)

No ordinary work done by a man is either as hard or as responsible as the work of a woman who is bringing up a family of small children; for upon her time and strength demands are made, not only every hour of the day, but often every hour of the night. She may have to get up night after night to take care of a sick child, and yet must by day continue to do all her household duties as well; and if the family means are scant, she must usually enjoy even her rare holidays taking her whole brood of children with her.

The birth pangs make all men the debtors of all women. Above all, our sympathy and regard are due to the struggling wives among those whom Abraham Lincoln called the plain people, and whom he so loved and trusted; for the lives of these women are often led on the lonely heights of quiet, self-sacrificing heroism.

—THEODORE ROOSEVELT, FROM A SPEECH TO THE NATIONAL CONGRESS
OF MOTHERS IN WASHINGTON, D.C., ON MARCH 13, 1905

Photographed in 1923 in a Washington ballroom, these marathon
dancers had just reached the 40-hour mark.

The harder you work, the harder it is to surrender.

—Football coach Vince Lombardi, from his book *Winning is
the Only Thing* (The World Publishing Company, 1970)

Perseverance is the
keynote to success.

—AMERICAN PROVERB

*There is no substitute
for hard work.*

—THOMAS ALVA EDISON
(1847–1931)

IT COULDN'T
BE DONE

Somebody said that it couldn't
be done,
But he with a chuckle replied
That maybe it couldn't, but he
would be one
Who wouldn't say so till he'd
tried.

—EDGAR ALBERT GUEST
(1881–1959)

I learned this, at least, by my experiment: that if one advances confidently in the direction of his dreams, and endeavors to live the life which he has imagined, he will meet with a success unexpected in common hours. He will put some things behind, will pass an invisible boundary; new, universal, and more liberal laws will begin to establish themselves around and within him; or the old laws be expanded, and interpreted in his favor in a more liberal sense, and he will live with the license of a higher order of beings. In proportion as he simplifies his life, the laws of the universe will appear less complex, and solitude will not be solitude, nor poverty poverty, nor weakness weakness. If you have built castles in the air, your work need not be lost; that is where they should be. Now put the foundations under them.

—HENRY DAVID THOREAU, FROM HIS MASTERWORK *WALDEN; OR, LIFE IN THE WOODS* (1854), A SERIES OF 18 ESSAYS WRITTEN DURING HIS TWO-YEAR EXPERIMENT IN "BASIC LIVING" AT WALDEN POND, NEAR CONCORD, MASSACHUSETTS

Stick to your aim; the mongrel's
    hold will slip,
But only crow-bars loose the
    bull-dog's lip;
Small as he looks, the jaw that
    never yields,
Drags down the bellowing
    monarch of the fields.

—OLIVER WENDELL HOLMES
    (1809–1894), FROM
    ENCYCLOPAEDIA OF QUOTATIONS
    (DAVID MCKAY, 1894)

*Perseverance will
accomplish all things.*

—AMERICAN PROVERB

Keep the faculty of effort alive in you by a little gratuitous exercise every day. That is, be systematically ascetic or heroic in little unnecessary points, do every day or two something for no other reason than that you would rather not do it, so that when the hour of dire need draws nigh, it may find you not unnerved and untrained to stand the test.

—WILLIAM JAMES (1842–1910), FROM HIS *PRINCIPLES OF PSYCHOLOGY*

THE STEADFAST TIN SOLDIER

— A RETELLING

This simple story serves to remind us that, although we often cannot control the events that govern our lives, remaining true to our goals is what matters most of all.

Once upon a time, there were twenty-five tin soldiers in a wooden box. Each was brave. Each was handsome and wore a smart, blue uniform. One soldier, Will, had only a single leg. He had been made last, and the toy maker had run out of tin. Will stood just as straight on his one leg as the others did on two, and he was just as brave and handsome.

The tin soldiers were given to a boy on his birthday. Will looked around and found that he was in a nursery. There were many other toys in the room. On the far side of the table, he saw a castle made of paper. In the doorway of the castle stood a beautiful paper maiden. Will fell in love with her at once.

The paper maiden, whose name was Alyssa, was a very graceful dancer. One arm was raised above her head, and one foot was lifted so high behind her that Will thought she had only one leg, just like him. She wore a dress made of sky blue gauze with a blue ribbon on one sleeve. "She would make a perfect wife for me," thought Will. He gazed and gazed at the paper maiden, unable to take his eyes off her.

Evening came, and the boy put all the soldiers except Will back in the box. The tin soldier stood stiffly at attention and watched Alyssa. She stood still and looked at him out of the corner of her eye.

The next morning the boy took the soldier and stood him on the windowsill. All of a sudden, a gust of wind blew. Will fell out of the window, and his hat stuck in the dirt between stones in the street below.

Soon it began to rain. The rain came down so hard that water ran in torrents down the street. Will bravely waited for the downpour to end. When it was over, two boys found the toy soldier. They made a paper boat, put Will in it, and floated him down a canal.

The canal emptied into a dark tunnel. The waters were so swift that the paper boat whirled and tipped dangerously, but the tin soldier held fast and was very brave. How he wished that the beautiful Alyssa could be here with him! Then he would have been happy.

A big rat who lived in the tunnel suddenly loomed up beside the boat. "Where is your pass?" the rat demanded. "Give me your pass at once."

The tin soldier remained still and steady. The rat swam as fast as he could, but the boat whirled away too fast in the current.

Soon the rat was left behind. Will let out a great sigh of relief.

Will wondered what was in store for him next and if he would ever see the beautiful Alyssa again. The current grew stronger and stronger, pulling the boat along faster and faster. Just as Will began to see daylight at the end of the tunnel, he heard a terrible splashing. Will's boat was heading straight for a waterfall.

He knew the poor, soggy boat could never survive a waterfall, but there was no avoiding it. "This must certainly be my end," thought the tin soldier as he plunged swiftly down into the whirlpool. "I will never again see the beautiful Alyssa, nor will I ever know how wonderful it would have been to watch her dance for me."

Round and round he whirled. His shiny blue uniform caught the eye of a large fish. The fish stopped, looked Will over from head to toe, and then swallowed him in one gulp. It was much darker in the fish than in the tunnel, but Will held himself as straight as he could.

After a long time there was a flash like lightning, and Will saw daylight again. The fish had been caught on someone's hook. Now it was in a kitchen, and the cook was preparing it for dinner.

"My goodness! Look at this tin soldier inside my fish!" exclaimed the cook. She pulled Will out, then wiped him off and brought him to the same nursery he was in before.

Will looked around and saw the box where his brothers were and the paper castle. His heart started to beat faster when he realized that he was home. The boy came into the nursery and looked at the tin soldier.

"Where have you been?" the little boy asked him in an accusing tone. "You're damp, and you smell like a fish." Suddenly he opened the window and tossed Will into the flower garden below. Will lay among the petunias and felt sad, but he remained brave.

Just then a gentle wind blew over him. It blew through the house, caught up Alyssa, and blew her straight out the open window into the garden. With a graceful little flutter, the paper dancer landed next to Will among the petunias.

The two looked at each other with beating hearts and adoring eyes. Then they slid very close together.

"Will you stay with me and be my wife?" Will asked.

"Yes, for- ever and ever!" she whispered.

I will demand a commitment to excellence and to victory,
and that is what life is all about.

—FOOTBALL COACH VINCE LOMBARDI, FROM HIS BOOK *WINNING IS*
THE ONLY THING (THE WORLD PUBLISHING COMPANY, 1970)

I believe that man will not merely endure; he will prevail. He is immortal, not because he alone among creatures has an inexhaustible voice, but because he has a soul, a spirit capable of compassion and sacrifice and endurance. The poet's, the writer's, duty is to write about these things. It is his privilege to help man endure by lifting his heart, by reminding him of the courage and honor and hope and pride and compassion and pity and sacrifice which have been the glory of his past. The poet's voice need not merely be the record of man, it can be one of the props, the pillars to help him endure and prevail.

—WILLIAM FAULKNER, FROM A SPEECH HE DELIVERED AFTER BEING AWARDED THE NOBEL PRIZE FOR LITERATURE ON DECEMBER 10, 1950

INSCRIPTION ON PLYMOUTH ROCK MONUMENT

This monument marks the first burying ground in Plymouth of the passengers of the *Mayflower*. Here, under cover of darkness, the fast dwindling company laid their dead, leveling the earth above them lest the Indians should learn how many were the graves. History records no nobler venture for faith and freedom than of this Pilgrim band. In weariness and painfulness, in watching often in hunger and cold, they laid the foundation of a state wherein every man through countless ages should have liberty to worship God in his own way. May their example inspire thee to do thy part in perpetuating and spreading the lofty ideals of our republic throughout the world.

They laid the foundation of a state wherein every man through countless ages should have liberty.

Heroism, the mountaineers say, is endurance for one moment more.

—JOURNALIST GEORGE KENNAN (1845–1924), IN A LETTER TO A FRIEND

Traveling with me you find what never tires.
The earth never tires,
The earth is rude, silent, incomprehensible at first, Nature is
rude and incomprehensible at first,
Be not discouraged, keep on, there are divine things well
envelop'd,
I swear to you there are divine things more beautiful than
words can tell.

—WALT WHITMAN, FROM *LEAVES OF GRASS* (1855)

The whole history of the progress of human liberty shows that all concessions yet made to her august claims have been born of earnest struggle. . . . If there is no struggle, there is no progress. Those who profess to favor freedom, and yet deprecate agitation, are men who want crops without plowing up the ground, they want rain without thunder and lightning. They want the ocean without the awful roar of its many waters.

—FREDERICK DOUGLASS (1817–1895)

The Mothers of our Forest-Land!
   Stout-hearted dames were they;
With nerve to wield the battle-brand,
   And join the border-fray.
Our rough land had no braver,
   In its days of blood and strife—
Aye ready for severest toil,
   Aye free to peril life.

—EXCERPT FROM "THE MOTHERS OF THE WEST," BY WILLIAM D. GALLAGHER; FROM *POEMS OF AMERICAN HISTORY* (HOUGHTON MIFFLIN CO., 1950)

CAN'T

How history repeats itself
   You'll say when you remember Grant,
Who, in his boyhood days, once sought
   Throughout the lexicon for "can't."

He could not find the word that day,
   The earnest boy whose name was Grant;
He never found it through long years,
   With all their power to disenchant.

No hostile host could give him pause;
   Rivers and mountains could not daunt;
He never found that hindering word—
   The steadfast man whose name was Grant.

—HARRIET PRESCOTT SPOFFORD (1835–1921), PAYING HOMAGE TO CIVIL WAR GENERAL ULYSSES S. GRANT

MOLLY PITCHER

Her real name was Mary Ludwig, but she became known as Molly Pitcher because she served pitchers of cold water to thirsty soldiers during the Revolutionary War. The following poem, written by Laura E. Richards (1850–1943), celebrates the heroism Molly displayed at the Battle of Monmouth, where she took the place of her artilleryman-husband after he collapsed from heat exhaustion.

All day the great guns barked and roared;
   All day the big balls screeched and soared;
All day, 'mid the sweating gunners grim,
Who toiled in their smoke-shroud dense and dim,
Sweet Molly labored with courage high,
With steady hand and watchful eye,
Till the day was ours, and the sinking sun
Looked down on the field of Monmouth won,
And Molly standing beside her gun.

Now, Molly, rest your weary arm!
Safe, Molly, all is safe from harm.
Now, woman, bow your aching head,
And weep in sorrow o'er your dead!

Next day on that field so hardly won,
Stately and calm stands Washington,
And looks where our gallant Greene doth lead
A figure clad in motley weed—
A soldier's cap and a soldier's coat
Masking a woman's petticoat.
He greets our Molly in kindly wise;
He bids her raise her tearful eyes;
And now he hails her before them all
Comrade and soldier, whate'er befall,
"And since she has played a man's full part,
A man's reward for her loyal heart!
And Sergeant Molly Pitcher's name
Be writ henceforth on the shield of fame!"

Oh, Molly, with your eyes so blue!
Oh, Molly, Molly, here's to you!
Sweet honor's roll will aye be richer
To hold the name of Molly Pitcher.

F rom dusk till dawn the livelong night
    She kept the tallow dips alight,
And fast her nimble fingers flew
To sew the stars upon the blue.
With weary eyes and aching head
She stitched the stripes of white and red,
And when the day came up the stair
Complete across a carven chair
    Hung Betsy's battle flag.

—EXCERPT FROM "BETSY'S BATTLE FLAG," BY
MINNA IRVING; FROM *POEMS OF AMERICAN
HISTORY* (HOUGHTON MIFFLIN CO., 1950)

I preach to you, then, my countrymen, that our country calls not for the life of ease, but for the life of strenuous endeavor. The twentieth century looms before us big with the fate of many nations. If we stand idly by, if we seek merely swollen, slothful ease, and ignoble peace, if we shrink from the hard contests where men must win at hazard of their lives and at the risk of all they hold dear, then the bolder and stronger peoples will pass us by and will win for themselves the domination of the world.

Let us therefore boldly face the life of strife, resolute to do our duty well and manfully; resolute to uphold righteousness by deed and by word; resolute to be both honest and brave, to serve high ideals, yet to use practical methods. Above all, let us shrink from no strife, moral or physical, within or without the nation, provided we are certain that the strife is justified; for it is only through strife, through hard and dangerous endeavor, that we shall ultimately win the goal of true national greatness.

— THEODORE ROOSEVELT, FROM A SPEECH IN 1900

L et us contemplate our forefathers, and posterity, and resolve to maintain the rights bequeathed to us from the former, for the sake of the latter. The necessity of the times, more than ever, calls for our utmost circumspection, deliberation, fortitude and perseverance. Let us remember that "if we suffer tamely a lawless attack upon our liberty, we encourage it, and involve others in our doom." It is a very serious consideration... that millions yet unborn may be the miserable sharers of the event.

— SAMUEL ADAMS, FROM A SPEECH IN 1771

THE BATTLE OF TRENTON

*This poem, by an unknown author, celebrates a spectacular Revolutionary
War victory by American troops in 1776. After crossing the ice-covered
Delaware River by boat, George Washington's army surprised some
1,200 Hessian troops loyal to the British, taking most of them prisoner
while sustaining only four casualties.*

On Christmas-day in seventy-six,
Our ragged troops, with bayonets fixed,
   For Trenton marched away.
The Delaware see! the boats below!
The light obscured by hail and snow!
   But no signs of dismay.

Our object was the Hessian band,
That dared invade fair freedom's land,
   And quarter in that place.
Great Washington he led us on,
Whose streaming flag, in storm or sun,
   Had never known disgrace.

In silent march we passed the night,
Each soldier panting for the fight,
   Though quite benumbed with frost.
Greene on the left at six began,
The right was led by Sullivan
   Who ne'er a moment lost.

Their pickets stormed, the alarm was spread,
That rebels risen from the dead
   Were marching into town.
Some scampered here, some scampered there,
And some for action did prepare;
   But soon their arms laid down.

Twelve hundred servile miscreants,
With all their colors, guns, and tents,
   Were trophies of the day.
The frolic o'er, the bright canteen,
In centre, front, and rear was seen
   Driving fatigue away.

Now, brothers of the patriot bands,
Let's sing deliverance from the hands
   Of arbitrary sway.
And as our life is but a span,
Let's touch the tankard while we can,
   In memory of that day.

—FROM *POEMS OF AMERICAN HISTORY* (HOUGHTON MIFFLIN CO., 1950)

Loyalty

A person can be loyal to many things: one's country, a special cause or ideal, a cherished institution, another person, or even a favorite product. Loyalty to one's country—patriotism, in a word—is perhaps its loftiest manifestation, for it reflects a devotion to one's entire society and way of life, a devotion for which many, when called upon, have dutifully laid down their lives.

When we read some of the patriotic sentiments expressed by early Americans—particularly those who participated in the struggle for independence—their allegiance is often so passionate and unswerving that it borders on religious zealotry. It is not by coincidence that the name of God is evoked in so many of their writings and speeches. Like religious faith, loyalty is based on trust and love, and it assumes a willingness to make sacrifices to achieve a greater good.

Also like faith, loyalty holds the promise of future rewards. Revolutionary War patriot Elias Boudinot put it in the form of a question: "Who knows but the country for which we have fought and bled may hereafter become a theatre of greater events than yet have been known to mankind?"

On July 21, 1776, Abigail Adams wrote a letter to her husband, John Adams, describing to the future President the celebration in Boston following the formal adoption of the Declaration of Independence.

Last Thursday, after hearing a very good sermon, I went with the multitude into King Street to hear the Proclamation for Independence read and proclaimed. Some field-pieces with the train were brought there. The troops appeared under arms, and all the inhabitants assembled there (the small-pox prevented many thousands from the country), when Colonel Crafts read from the balcony of the State House the proclamation. Great attention was given to every word. As soon as he ended, the cry from the balcony was, "God save our American States," and then three cheers which rent the air. The bells rang, the privateers fired, the forts and batteries, the cannon were discharged, the platoons followed, and every face appeared joyful. Mr. Bowdoin then gave a sentiment, "Stability and perpetuity to American independence." After

dinner, the King's Arms were taken down from the State House, and every vestige of him from every place in which it appeared, and burnt in King Street. Thus ends royal authority in this State. And all the people shall say Amen.

—From *The American Reader* (Paul M. Angle, 1958)

Victory is certain!…
Trust in God and fear not!
And remember the Alamo,
remember the Alamo!

—SAM HOUSTON, ADDRESSING HIS
TEXAS TROOPS ON APRIL 21,
1836, SEVERAL HOURS BEFORE
THEY MET AND DEFEATED THE
FORCES OF MEXICAN GENERAL
SANTA ANNA

Excerpt from a letter written by diplomat (and future President) John Adams to his wife Abigail on July 3, 1776.

I am well aware of the toil, and blood, and treasure, that it will cost us to maintain this [Declaration of Independence], and support and defend these States. Yet, through all the gloom, I can see the rays of ravishing light and glory. I can see that the end is more than worth all the means, and that posterity will triumph in that day's transaction, even although we should rue it, which I trust in God we shall not.

—FROM *COLONIES TO NATION, 1763–1789* (W. W. NORTON & CO., 1975)

After signing the [surrender] papers, [General] Grant introduced Lee to his staff. As he shook hands with Grant's military secretary Ely Parker, a Seneca Indian, Lee stared a moment at Parker's dark features and said, "I am glad to see one real American here." Parker responded, "We are all Americans."

—JAMES M. McPHERSON, FROM *BATTLE CRY OF FREEDOM* (OXFORD UNIVERSITY PRESS, 1988)

A MATTER OF HONOR

What is patriotism? Is it a narrow affection for the spot where a man was born? Are the very clods where we tread entitled to this ardent preference because they are greener? No, sir, this is not the character of the virtue, and it soars higher for its object. It is an extended self-love, mingling with all the enjoyments of life, and twisting itself with the minutest filaments of the heart. It is thus we obey the laws of society, because they are the laws of virtue. In their authority we see not the array of force and terror, but the venerable image of our country's honor. Every good citizen makes that honor his own, and cherishes it not only as precious but as sacred. He is willing to risk his life in its defence, and is conscious that he gains protection while he gives it. For what rights of a citizen will be deemed inviolable when a state renounces the principles that constitute their security? Or, if his life should not be invaded, what would its enjoyments be in a country odious to the eyes of strangers and dishonored in his own? Could he look with affection and veneration to such a country as his parent? The sense of having one would die within him; he would blush for his patriotism, if he retained any, and justly, for it would be a vice. He would be a banished man in his native land.

—STATESMAN AND ESSAYIST FISHER AMES (1758–1808),
FROM *WORKS OF FISHER AMES* (1854)

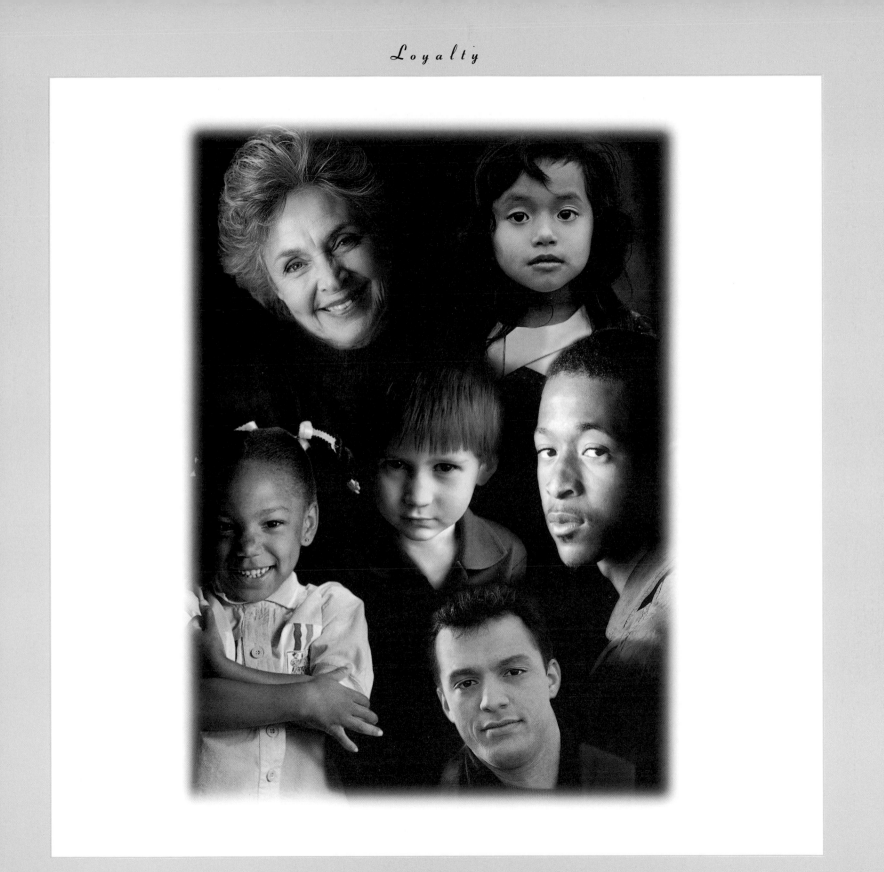

GOD BLESS AMERICA

God bless America,
Land that I love,
Stand beside her and guide her
Through the night with a light
    from above;
From the mountains, to the
    prairies,
To the oceans white with foam,
God bless America, My home
    sweet home,
God bless America, My home
    sweet home.

—IRVING BERLIN, 1938

We must be ready to dare all for our country. For history does not long entrust the care of freedom to the weak or the timid. We must acquire proficiency in defense and display stamina in purpose.

We must be willing, individually and as a nation, to accept whatever sacrifices may be required of us. A people that values its privileges above its principles soon loses both.

These basic precepts are not lofty abstractions, far removed from matters of daily living. They are laws of spiritual strength that generate and define our material strength. Patriotism means equipped forces and prepared citizenry. Moral stamina means more energy and more productivity, on the farm and in the factory. Love of liberty means the guarding of every resource that makes freedom possible—from the sanctity of our families and the wealth of our soil to the genius of our scientists.

—DWIGHT D. EISENHOWER, FROM HIS
INAUGURAL ADDRESS ON JANUARY 20, 1953

THE MARINES' SONG

From the Halls of Montezuma
To the shores of Tripoli
We fight our country's battles
On the land as on the sea.
First to fight for right and freedom
And to keep our honor clean;
We are proud to claim the title
Of United States Marines.

Our flag's unfurled to every breeze
From dawn to setting sun;
We have fought in every clime and place
Where we could take a gun.
In the snow of far-off Northern lands
And in sunny tropic scenes;
You will find us always on the job—
The United States Marines.

Here's health to you and to our Corps
Which we are proud to serve;
In many a strife we've fought for life
And never lost our nerve.
If the Army and the Navy
Ever look on Heaven's scenes,
They will find the streets are guarded
By United States Marines.

—AUTHOR UNKNOWN (CIRCA 1875)

Who knows but the country for which we have fought and bled may hereafter become a theatre of greater events than yet have been known to mankind?

May these invigorating prospects lead us to the exercise of every virtue, religious, moral, and political. May we be roused to a circumspect conduct, to an exact obedience to the laws of our own making, to the preservation of the spirit and principles of our truly invaluable Constitution, to respect and attention to magistrates of our own choice; and finally, by our example as well as precept, add to the real happiness of our fellow-men and the particular glory of our common country.

—REVOLUTIONARY WAR PATRIOT ELIAS BOUDINOT (1740–1821)

Our American past compared to that of any European country has a character all its own. Its peculiarity consists, not merely in its brevity but in the fact that from the beginning it has been informed by an idea. From the beginning Americans have been anticipating and projecting a better future. From the beginning the land of democracy has been figured as the land of promise. Thus the American's loyalty to the national tradition rather affirms than denies the imaginative projection of a better future.

An America which was not the land of promise, which was not informed by a prophetic outlook and a more or less constructive ideal, would not be the America bequeathed to us by our forefathers. In cherishing the promise of a better national future, the American is fulfilling rather than imperiling the substance of the national tradition....

—HERBERT CROLY, FOUNDER OF THE *NEW REPUBLIC*,
FROM HIS BOOK *THE PROMISE OF AMERICAN LIFE* (1909)

BATTLE HYMN OF THE REPUBLIC

Julia Ward Howe (1819–1910), a suffragist and social reformer, wrote the lyrics to this well-known song on November 18, 1861. Although Union forces quickly adopted it as a marching song, it eventually gained nationwide popularity and was sung by American troops in the Spanish-American War, World War I, and World War II.

Mine eyes have seen the glory
    of the coming of the Lord;
He is trampling out the vintage
    where the grapes of wrath are stored;
He hath loosed the fateful lightning
    of His terrible swift sword:
His truth is marching on.

I have seen Him in the watch-fires
    of a hundred circling camps;
They have builded Him an altar
    in the evening dews and damps;
I can read His righteous sentence
    by the dim and flaring lamps:
His day is marching on.

I have read a fiery gospel
    writ in burnished rows of steel:
"As ye deal with my contemners,
    so with you my grace shall deal;
Let the Hero, born of woman,
    crush the serpent with his heel,
Since God is marching on."

He has sounded forth the trumpet
    that shall never call retreat;
He is sifting out the hearts of men
    before His judgement-seat:
Oh, be swift, my soul to answer Him!
    be jubilant, my feet!
Our God is marching on.

In the beauty of the lilies
    Christ was born across the sea,
With a glory in his bosom
    that transfigures you and me:
As he died to make men holy,
    let us die to make men free,
While God is marching on.

Washington, D.C., lawyer Francis Scott Key wrote the lyrics to "The Star-Spangled Banner" on September 14, 1814, as he observed a British naval assault on the city of Baltimore. The melody is attributed to British composer John Stafford Smith. The first verse of the song was officially adopted as the national anthem of the United States on March 3, 1931.

THE STAR-SPANGLED BANNER

 say can you see by the dawn's early light
   What so proudly we hail'd at the twilight's last gleaming,
Whose broad stripes & bright stars through the perilous fight
   O'er the ramparts we watch'd, were so gallantly streaming?
   And the rocket's red glare, the bombs bursting in air,
   Gave proof through the night that our flag was still there,
O say does that star-spangled banner yet wave
O'er the land of the free & the home of the brave?

On the shore dimly seen through the mists of the deep,
    Where the foe's haughty host in dread silence reposes,
What is that which the breeze, o'er the towering steep,
    As it fitfully blows, half conceals, half discloses?
    Now it catches the gleam of the morning's first beam
    In full glory reflected now shines in the stream
'Tis the star-spangled banner—O long may it wave
O'er the land of the free & the home of the brave!

And where is that band who so vauntingly swore,
    That the havoc of war & the battle's confusion
A home & a Country should leave us no more?
    Their blood has wash'd out their foul footstep's pollution.
    No refuge could save the hireling & slave
    From the terror of flight or the gloom of the grave,
And the star-spangled banner in triumph doth wave
O'er the land of the free & the home of the brave.

O thus be it ever when freemen shall stand
    Between their lov'd home & the war's desolation!
Blest with vict'ry & peace may the heav'n rescued land
    Praise the power that hath made & preserv'd us a nation!
    Then conquer we must, when our cause it is just,
    And this be our motto—"In God is our Trust,"
And the star-spangled banner in triumph shall wave
O'er the land of the free & the home of the brave.

THE PLEDGE OF ALLEGIANCE

I pledge allegiance to the flag of the United States of America and to the Republic for which it stands, one Nation under God, indivisible, with liberty and justice for all.

THE FLAG GOES BY

Inspired by the patriotic fervor surrounding the Spanish-American War,
Henry Holcomb Bennett wrote these once-popular lyrics in 1898.

Hats off!
Along the street there comes
A blare of bugles, a ruffle of drums,
A flash of color beneath the sky:
Hats off!
The flag is passing by!

Blue and crimson and white it shines,
Over the steel-tipped, ordered lines.
Hats off!
The colors before us fly;
But more than the flag is passing by.

Sea-fights and land-fights, grim and great,
Fought to make and to save the state:
Weary marches and sinking ships;
Cheers of victory on dying lips;

Days of plenty and years of peace;
March of a strong land's swift increase;
Equal justice, right and law,
Stately honor and reverend awe;

Sign of a nation, great and strong
To ward her people from foreign wrong:
Pride and glory and honor—all
Live in the colors to stand or fall.

Hats off!
Along the street there comes
A blare of bugles, a ruffle of drums;
And loyal hearts are beating high:
Hats off!
The flag is passing by!

AMERICANS BY CHOICE

We have gathered here to affirm a faith, a faith in a common purpose, a common conviction, a common devotion. Some of us have chosen America as the land of our adoption; the rest have come from those who did the same. For this reason we have some right to consider ourselves a picked group, a group of those who had the courage to break from the past and brave the dangers and the loneliness of a strange land. What was the object that nerved us, or those who went before us, to this choice? We sought liberty: freedom from oppression, freedom from want, freedom to be ourselves.

—JURIST LEARNED HAND (1872–1961), FROM A SPEECH IN NEW YORK DURING "I AM AN AMERICAN DAY" FESTIVITIES ON MAY 21, 1944

THE MEANING OF PATRIOTISM

On July 4, 1828, social reformer and lecturer Frances (Fanny) Wright (1795–1852) presented what is believed to be the first public Independence Day oration by a woman. She took the opportunity to urge Americans to favor patriotism from a global perspective, embracing all of humankind, as opposed to the traditional, nationalistic kind of patriotism that favors one's own country above all others.

Patriotism, in the exclusive meaning, is surely not made for America. Mischievous everywhere, it were here both mischievous and absurd. The very origin of the people is opposed to it. The institutions, in their principle, militate against it. The day we are celebrating protests against it.

It is for Americans, more especially, to nourish a nobler sentiment; one more consistent with their origin, and more conducive to their future improvement. It is for them, more especially, to know why they love their country; and to *feel* that they love it, not because it *is* their country, but because it is the palladium of human liberty—the favored scene of human improvement. It is for them, more especially, to examine their institutions; and to *feel* that they honor them because they are based on just principles. It is for them, more especially, to examine their institutions, because they have the means of improving them; to examine their laws, because at will they can alter them. It is for them to lay aside luxury whose wealth is in industry; idle parade whose strength is in knowledge; ambitious distinctions whose principle is equality. It is for them not to rest, satisfied with words, who can seize upon things; and to remember that equality means, not the mere equality of political rights, however valuable, but equality of instruction and equality in virtue; and that liberty means, not the mere voting at elections, but the free and fearless exercise of the mental faculties and that self-possession which springs out of well-reasoned opinions and consistent practice. It is for them to honor principles rather than men—to commemorate events rather than days; when they rejoice, to know for what they rejoice, and to rejoice only for what has brought and what brings peace and happiness to men.

The event that we commemorate this day has procured much of both, and shall procure in the onward course of human improvement more than we can now conceive of. For this—for the good obtained and yet in store for our race—let us rejoice!

THE STARS AND STRIPES FOREVER

Written by John Philip Sousa during the 1890s, "The Stars and Stripes Forever" was one of the most popular marching songs of that period. Saved as the traditional closing piece for all of Sousa's concerts, it is still a favorite of marching bands today.

Let martial note in triumph float,
　　And liberty extend its mighty hand.
A flag appears, 'mid thund'rous cheers,
The banner of the Western land.
The emblem of the brave and true,
Its folds protect no tyrant crew,
The red and white and starry blue
Is freedom's shield and hope.

Other nations may deem their flags the best,
And cheer them with fervid elation.
But the flag of the North and South and West
Is the flag of flags, the flag of freedom's nation.

Chorus:
Let eagle shriek from lofty peak
The never-ending watchword of our land.

Let summer breeze waft through the trees
The echo of the chorus grand.
Sing out for liberty and light,
Sing out for freedom and the right.
Sing out for Union and its might,
Oh, patriotic sons!

Hurrah for the flag of the free;
May it wave as our standard forever.
The gem of the land and the sea,
The banner of the right.
Let despots remember the day
When our fathers, with mighty endeavor,
Proclaimed as they marched to the fray,
That by their might, and by their right, it
　　　waves forever!

Other nations may deem their flags the best,
And cheer them with fervid elation.
But the flag of the North and South and West
Is the flag of flags, the flag of freedom's nation.

Courage

From the very beginning, America has been the "home of the brave," a place where men and women could make a life for themselves if they were willing to face the obstacles. What distinguishes courageous Americans is their pioneering spirit, their willingness to seek out and explore new frontiers—not just in the traditional sense of acquiring new lands, but also in the sciences, in business, and even in the arts.

Courage allows us to proceed boldly in life, but the very process of doing so increases the chances that we may encounter unexpected obstacles or fall into harm's way. "Courage is the price that Life exacts for granting peace," wrote aviator Amelia Earhart. Another legend of aviation, Charles A. Lindbergh, echoed these sentiments in his autobiography *The Spirit of St. Louis*. "A certain amount of danger," he said, "is essential to the quality of life."

When we read the brave words of Lieutenant Colonel William Travis, commander of American troops at the ill-fated Alamo, pledging to "die like a soldier," we cannot help but be moved, but no less inspiring are the words of blind and deaf author Helen Keller, who shows us that true courage is also born of ordinary, everyday circumstances.

Following is the text of a letter written by George Washington to his mother Mary on July 18, 1755. Only 23 years old at the time, Washington was recovering from an unsuccessful military expedition to the Ohio Valley to take Fort Duquesne (formerly Fort Cumberland) from the French.

Undated painting of George
Washington by Gilbert Stuart
(1755–1828)

Honour'd Mad'm:

As I doubt not but you have heard of our defeat, and perhaps have it represented in a worse light (if possible) than it deserves; I have taken this earliest oppertunity to give you some acct. of the Engagement, as it happen'd within 7 miles of the French Fort, on Wednesday the 9th. Inst.

We March'd on to that place with't any considerable loss, having only now and then a stragler pick'd up by the French Scoutg. Ind'nd. When we came there, we were attack'd by a Body of French and Indns. whose number, (I am certain) did not exceed 300 Men; our's consisted of abt. 1,300 well arm'd Troops; chiefly of the English Soldiers, who were struck with such a panick, that they behav'd with more cowardice than it is possible to conceive; The Officers behav'd Gallantly in order to encourage their Men, for which they suffer'd greatly; there being near 60 kill'd and wounded; a large proportion out of the number we had! The Virginia Troops shew'd a good deal of Bravery, and were near all kill'd; for I believe out of 3 Companys that were there, there is scarce 30 Men left alive; Capt. Peyrouny and all his Officer's down to a Corporal was kill'd; Capt. Polson shar'd near as hard a Fate; for only one of his was left: In short the dastardly behaviour of those they call regular's expos'd all others that were inclin'd to do their duty to almost certain death; and at last, in dispight of all the efforts of the Officer's to the Contrary, they broke and run as Sheep pursued by dogs; and it was impossible to rally them.

The Genl. was wounded; of w'ch he died 3 Days after; Sir Peter Halket was kill'd in the Field where died many other brave Officer's; I luckily escap'd with't a wound, tho' I had four Bullets through my Coat, and two Horses shot under me; Captns. Orme and Morris two of the

Genls. Aids de Camp, were wounded early in the Engagem't. which render'd the duty hard upon me, as I was the only person then left to distribute the Genl's. Orders which I was scarcely able to do, as I was not half recover'd from a violent illness, that confin'd me to my Bed, and a Waggon, for above 10 Days; I am still in a weak and Feeble cond'n; which induces me to halt here, 2 or 3 Days in hopes of recov'g. a little Strength, to enable me to proceed homewards; from whence, I fear I shall not be able to stir till towards Sept., so that I shall not have the pleasure of seeing you till then, unless it be in Fairfax; please to give my love to Mr. Lewis and my Sister, and Compts. to Mr. Jackson and all other Fds. that enquire after me. I am, Hon'd Madam Yr. most dutiful Son.

P.S. You may acqt. Priscilla Mullican that her Son Charles is very well, hav'g only rec'd a slight w'd in his Foot, w'ch will be cur'd with't detrimt. to him, in a very small time.

We had abt. 300 Men kill'd and as many, and more, wounded.

The enemy has demanded a surrender at discretion; otherwise the garrison are to be put to the sword if the fort is taken. I have answered the demand with a cannon shot, and our flag still waves proudly from the walls. *I shall never surrender nor retreat.* Then, I call on you in the name of liberty, of patriotism, and everything dear to the American character, to come to our aid with all dispatch. The enemy is receiving reinforcements daily and will no doubt increase to three or four thousand in four or five days. If this call is neglected, I am determined to sustain myself as long as possible and die like a soldier who never forgets what is due to his own honor and that of his country. Victory or Death.

—Lt. Col. William Barret Travis, commander
of American forces at the Alamo in 1836

COURAGE

Courage is armor
A blind man wears;
The calloused scar
Of outlived despairs:
Courage is Fear
That has said its prayers.

—Karle Wilson Baker

DOORS OF DARING

The mountains that inclose the vale
With walls of granite, steep and high,
Invite the fearless foot to scale
Their stairway toward the sky.

The restless, deep, dividing sea
That flows and foams from shore to shore,
Calls to its sunburned chivalry,
"Push out, set sail, explore!"

The bars of life at which we fret,
That seem to prison and control,
Are but the doors of daring, set
Ajar before the soul.

Say not, "Too poor," but freely give;
Sigh not, "Too weak," but boldly try;
You never can begin to live
Until you dare to die.

—CLERGYMAN AND EDUCATOR
HENRY VAN DYKE (1852–1933)

THE ROAD NOT TAKEN

Using ordinary, conversational language, poet Robert Frost (1874–1963) had a special talent for endowing rural imagery with symbolic and even metaphysical meaning, as he demonstrates here in this often cited work, which first appeared in his 1916 book Mountain Interval.

Two roads diverged in a yellow wood,
And sorry I could not travel both
And be one traveler, long I stood
And looked down one as far as I could
To where it bent in the undergrowth;

Then took the other, as just as fair,
And having perhaps the better claim,
Because it was grassy and wanted wear;
Though as for that, the passing there
Had worn them really about the same,

And both that morning equally lay
In leaves no step had trodden black.
Oh, I kept the first for another day!
Yet knowing how way leads on to way,
I doubted if I should ever come back.

I shall be telling this with a sigh
Somewhere ages and ages hence:
Two roads diverged in a wood, and I—
I took the one less traveled by,
And that has made all the difference.

Anyone familiar with the 1938 Metro-Goldwyn-Mayer production of The Wizard of Oz, *starring Judy Garland as Dorothy, will remember the following exchange, from the screenplay by Noel Langley, Florence Ryerson, and Edgar Allan Woolf (based on the original book by Lyman Frank Baum).*

DOROTHY to LION: Your majesty, if you were king, you wouldn't be afraid of anything?

LION: Not nobody! Not no how!

TIN MAN: Not even a rhinoceros?

LION: Imposserous!

DOROTHY: How about a hippopotamus?

LION: Why, I'd trash him from top to bottomus!

DOROTHY: Supposin' you met an elephant?

LION: I'd wrap him up in cellophant!

SCARECROW: What if it were a brontosaurus?

LION: I'd show him who was king of the forest!

DOROTHY, SCARECROW, and TIN MAN: How?

LION: How?! Courage!

 What makes a king out of a slave? Courage!

 What makes the flag on the mast to wave? Courage!

 What makes the elephant charge his tusk, in the misty mist, or the dusky dusk?

 What makes the muskrat guard his musk? Courage!

 What makes the Sphinx the seventh wonder? Courage!

 What makes the dawn come up like thunder? Courage!

 What makes the Hottentot so hot?

 What puts the 'ape' in apricot?

 What do they got that I ain't got?

DOROTHY, SCARECROW, and TIN MAN: Courage!

LION: You can say that again!

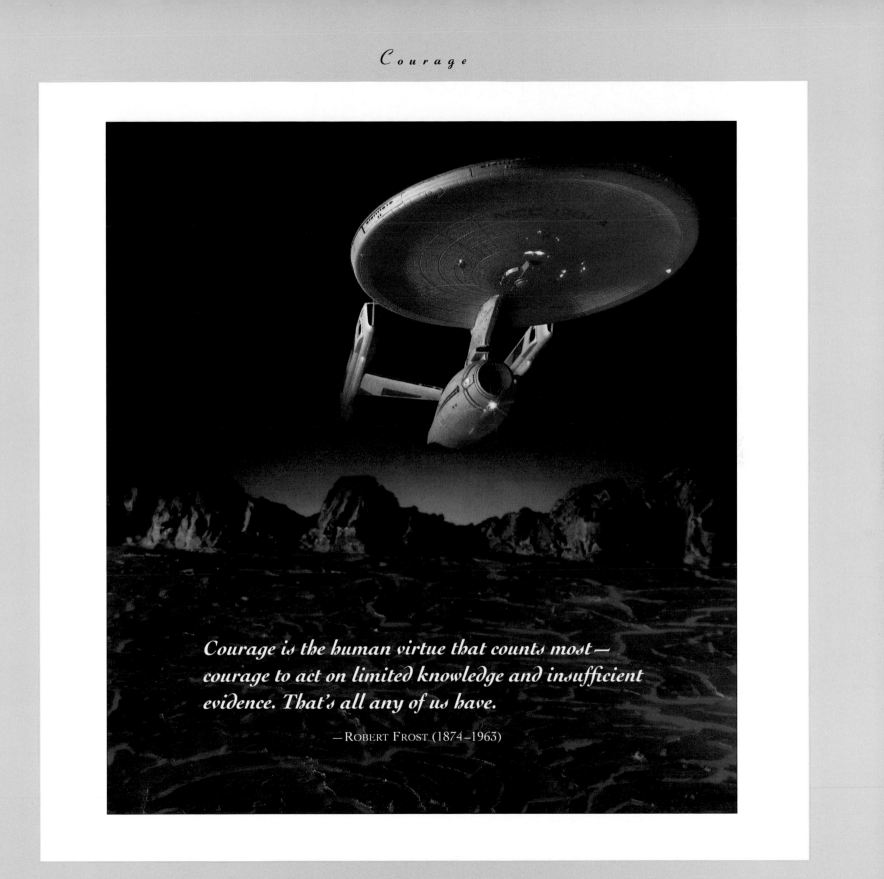

Courage is the human virtue that counts most— courage to act on limited knowledge and insufficient evidence. That's all any of us have.

—ROBERT FROST (1874–1963)

We deserve no earthly or heavenly blessing, for which we are unwilling to labor. For our part, we despise a freedom and equality obtained for us by others, and for which we have been unwilling to labor. A man who will not labor to gain his rights, is a man who would not, if he had them, prize and defend them.

—ABOLITIONIST FREDERICK
DOUGLASS (1817–1895)

The time is now near at hand which must probably determine, whether Americans are to be Freemen or Slaves; whether they are to have any property they can call their own; whether their Houses, and Farms, are to be pillaged and destroyed, and they consigned to a State of Wretchedness from which no human efforts will probably deliver them. The fate of unborn Millions will now depend, under God, on the Courage and Conduct of this army—Our cruel and unrelenting Enemy leaves us no choice but a brave resistance, or the most abject submission; this is all we can expect—We have therefore to resolve to conquer or die: Our own Country's Honor, all call upon us for a vigorous and manly exertion, and if we now shamefully fail, we shall become infamous to the whole world. Let us therefore rely upon the goodness of the Cause, and the aid of the supreme Being, in whose hands Victory is, to animate and encourage us to great and noble Actions—The Eyes of all our Countrymen are now upon us, and we shall have their blessings, and praises, if happily we are the instruments of saving them from the Tyranny meditated against them. Let us therefore animate and encourage each other, and [show] the whole world, that a Freeman contending for Liberty on his own ground is superior to any slavish mercenary on earth.

—EXCERPTED FROM GENERAL ORDERS ISSUED BY GEORGE WASHINGTON
FROM HIS NEW YORK HEADQUARTERS ON JULY 2, 1776

WARREN'S ADDRESS AT BUNKER HILL, JUNE 16, 1775

—JOHN PIERPONT
(1785–1866)

A soldier and leader in the Revolutionary War, Joseph Warren was named a major general in the American Army on June 14, 1775. Three days later, he was killed at the Battle of Bunker Hill in Massachusetts.

Stand! the ground's your own,
    my braves!
Will ye give it up to slaves?
Will ye look for greener graves?
    Hope ye mercy still?
What's the mercy despots feel?
Hear it in that battle-peal!
Read it on yon bristling steel!
    Ask it—ye who will.

Fear ye foes who kill for hire?
Will ye to your homes retire?
Look behind you!—they're afire!
    And, before you, see
Who have done it! From the vale
On they come—and will ye quail?
Leaden rain and iron hail
    Let their welcome be!

In the God of battles trust!
Die we may—and die we must:
But, O, where can dust to dust
    Be consigned so well,
As where heaven its dews shall shed
On the martyred patriot's bed,
And the rocks shall raise their head,
    Of his deeds to tell?

OUR HEROES

Here's a hand to the boy who has courage
    To do what he knows to be right;
When he falls in the way of temptation,
    He has a hard battle to fight.
Who strives against self and his comrades
    Will find a most powerful foe.
All honor to him if he conquers.
    A cheer for the boy who says "NO!"

There's many a battle fought daily
    The world knows nothing about;
There's many a brave little soldier
    Whose strength puts a legion to rout.
And he who fights sin singlehanded
    Is more of a hero, I say,
Than he who leads soldiers to battle
    And conquers by arms in the fray.

Be steadfast, my boy, when you're tempted,
    To do what you know to be right.
Stand firm by the colors of manhood,
    And you will o'ercome in the fight.
"The right," be your battle cry ever
    In waging the warfare of life,
And God, who knows who are the heroes,
    Will give you the strength for the strife.

—PHOEBE CARY (1824–1871)

Far better it is to dare mighty things, to win glorious triumphs, even though checkered by failure, than to take rank with those poor spirits who neither enjoy much nor suffer much, because they live in the gray twilight that knows not victory nor defeat.

—THEODORE ROOSEVELT, FROM A SPEECH
IN CHICAGO ON APRIL 10, 1899

OVER THERE

Over there, over there,
Send the word, send the word over there,
That the Yanks are coming, the Yanks are coming,
The drums rum-tumming everywhere.
So prepare, say a prayer,
Send the word, send the word to beware,
We'll be over, we're coming over,
And we won't come back till it's over over there.

—CHORUS FROM THE POPULAR SONG
BY GEORGE M. COHAN (1878–1942)

That's one small step for man, one giant leap for mankind.

—ASTRONAUT NEIL ARMSTRONG, AFTER STEPPING
ONTO THE MOON'S SURFACE ON JULY 20, 1969

THE PONY EXPRESS

The pony rider was usually a little bit of a man, brimful of spirit and endurance. No matter what time of the day or night his watch came on and no matter whether it was winter or summer, raining, snowing, hailing, or sleeting, or whether his beat was a level straight road or a crazy trail over mountain crags and precipices, or whether it led through peaceful regions or regions that swarmed with hostile Indians, he must be always ready to leap into the saddle and be off like the wind!

—MARK TWAIN, FROM *ROUGHING IT* (1871)

Pony Express Rider Under Attack by Indians
by Oscar Edmund Berninghaus (1874–1952)

A PORTRAIT OF COURAGE

Dolley Madison (1768–1849), American patriot and wife of James Madison, our fourth President, directed the evacuation of the White House in 1814 as British troops converged on the nation's capital during the waning months of the War of 1812.

Having already rescued many American treasures, Dolley did not want the Gilbert Stuart portrait of George Washington to fall into British possession. With cannons roaring and soldiers from both sides rushing about, Dolley ordered the picture to be taken down. Working quickly, and with much effort, it was removed and sent off to a safe place. Shortly after the White House was abandoned, the British took control of the building and set it on fire. Dolley wrote about the day's events to her sister:

"Three o'clock. Will you believe it, my sister? We have had a battle, or skirmish, near Bladensburg, and here I am still, within sound of the cannon! Mr. Madison comes not. May God protect us! Two messengers, covered with dust, come to bid me fly; but here I means to wait for him.... I insist on waiting until the large picture of George Washington is secured, and it requires it to be unscrewed from the wall. This process was found to be too tedious for these perilous moments; I have ordered the frame to be broken, and the canvas taken out. It is done? ... And now my dear sister, I must leave this house, or the retreating army will make me a prisoner in it by filling up the road I am directed to take. When I shall again write to you, or where I shall be tomorrow, I cannot tell."

A celebrated aviator, Amelia Earhart was the first woman to fly alone across the Atlantic Ocean.

COURAGE

Courage is the price that Life exacts for
    granting peace.
The soul that knows it not
Knows no release from little things:
Knows not the livid loneliness of fear,
Nor mountain heights where bitter joy can hear
The sound of wings.

How can Life grant us boon of living, compensate
For dull gray ugliness and pregnant hate
Unless we dare
The soul's dominion? Each time we make a choice,
    we pay
With courage to behold resistless day,
And count it fair.

—AMELIA EARHART (1897–1937)

A'N'T I A WOMAN?

If de fust woman God ever made was strong enough to turn de world upside down all alone, dese women togedder (and she glanced her eye over the platform) ought to be able to turn it back, and get it right side up again! And now dey is asking to do it, de men better let'em.

—SOJOURNER TRUTH, ADDRESSING AN AMERICAN WOMEN'S RIGHTS CONVENTION IN AKRON, OHIO, IN 1851

Charles Lindbergh stands in front of his *Spirit of St. Louis*, the monoplane he used to make the first nonstop solo flight across the Atlantic Ocean (New York to Paris) on May 20–21, 1927.

But I didn't start on this flight to Paris because of its relative safety. I used that argument only to bolster my decision, and to convince people that the hazard wasn't too great. I'm not bound to carry the night mail. I'm not bound to be in aviation at all. I'm here only because I love the sky and flying more than anything else on earth. Of course there's danger; but a certain amount of danger is essential to the quality of life. I don't believe in taking foolish chances; but nothing can be accomplished without taking any chance at all.

—AVIATOR CHARLES A. LINDBERGH (1902–1974), FROM HIS 1953 AUTOBIOGRAPHY *THE SPIRIT OF ST. LOUIS* he *probability* that we may fall in the struggle *ought not* to deter us from the support of a cause we believe to be just; it *shall not* deter me. If ever I feel the soul within me elevate and expand to those dimensions not wholly unworthy of its Almighty Architect, it is when I contemplate the cause of my country, deserted by all the world beside, and I standing up boldly and alone and hurling defiance at her victorious oppressors. Here, without contemplating consequences, before High Heaven, and in the face of the world, I swear eternal fidelity to the just cause, as I deem it, of the land of my life, my liberty and my love. And who, that thinks with me, will not fearlessly adopt the oath that I take. Let none faulter, who thinks he is right, and we may succeed. But, if after all, we shall fail, be it so. We still shall have the proud consolation of saying to our consciences, and to the departed shade of our country's freedom, that the cause approved of our judgment, and adored of our hearts, in disaster, in chains, in torture, in death, we never faultered in defending.

—ABRAHAM LINCOLN, FROM A SPEECH IN THE ILLINOIS HOUSE OF REPRESENTATIVES ON DECEMBER 26, 1839

well-disciplined militia is a safe, an honorable guard to a community like this, whose inhabitants are by nature brave, and are laudably tenacious of that freedom in which they were born. From a well-regulated militia we have nothing to fear; their interest is the same with that of the state. When a country is invaded, the militia are ready to appear in its defence; they march into the field with that fortitude which a consciousness of the justice of their cause inspires; they do not jeopard their lives for a master who considers them only as the instruments of his ambition, and whom they regard only as the daily dispenser of the scanty pittance of bread and water.

No, they fight for their houses, their lands, for their wives, their children, for all who claim the tenderest names, and are held dearest in their hearts; they fight . . . for their liberty, and for themselves, and for their God.

—JOHN HANCOCK, FROM HIS "BOSTON MASSACRE ORATION" (1774)

TREE OF PARADISE

Despite being blind and deaf, Helen Keller (1880–1968) achieved remarkable success as an author, educator, and advocate of the handicapped. The following excerpt, from her 1902 book The Story of My Life, *is a moving account of the courage she showed in overcoming not only her physical limitations, but also her fears of a world she was only beginning to comprehend.*

Helen Keller (left) and her teacher Anne Sullivan. The photograph was taken in 1897, when Keller was 17 years old.

One day my teacher and I were returning from a long ramble. The morning had been fine, but it was growing warm and sultry when at last we turned our faces homeward. Two or three times we stopped to rest under a tree by the wayside. Our last halt was under a wild cherry tree a short distance from the house. The shade was grateful, and the tree was so easy to climb that I was able to scramble to a seat in the branches. It was so cool up in the tree that Miss Sullivan proposed that we have our luncheon there. I promised to keep still while she went to the house to fetch it.

Suddenly a change passed over the tree. All the sun's warmth left the air. I knew the sky was black, because all the heat, which meant light to me, had died out of the atmosphere. A strange odor came up from the earth. I knew it, it was the odor that always precedes a thunderstorm, and a nameless fear clutched at my heart. I felt absolutely alone, cut off from my friends and the firm earth. The immense, the unknown, enfolded me. I remained still and expectant; a chilling terror crept over me. I longed for my teacher's return; but above all things I wanted to get down from that tree.

There was a moment of sinister silence, then a multitudinous stirring of the leaves. A shiver ran through the tree, and the wind set forth a blast that would have knocked me off had I not clung to the branch with might and main. The tree swayed and strained. The small twigs snapped and fell about me in showers. A wild impulse to jump seized me, but terror held me fast. I crouched down in the fork of the tree. The branches lashed about me. I felt the intermittent jarring that came now and then, as if something heavy had fallen and the shock had traveled up till it reached the limb I sat on. It worked my suspense up to the highest point, and just as I was thinking the tree and I should fall together, my teacher seized my hand and helped me down. I clung to her, trembling with joy to feel the earth under my feet once more.

After this experience it was a long time before I climbed another tree. The mere thought filled me with terror. It was the sweet allurement of the mimosa tree in full bloom that finally overcame my fears. One beautiful summer morning when I was alone in the summer-house, reading, I became

aware of a wonderful subtle fragrance in the air. I started up and instinctively stretched out my hands. It seemed as if the spirit of spring had passed through the summer-house. "What is it?" I asked, and the next minute I recognized the odor of the mimosa blossoms. I felt my way to the end of the garden, knowing that the mimosa tree was near the fence, at the turn of the path. Yes, there it was, all quivering in the warm sunshine, its blossom-laden branches almost touching the long grass. Was there ever anything so exquisitely beautiful in the world before! Its delicate blossoms shrank from the slightest earthly touch; it seemed as if a tree of paradise had been transplanted to earth. I made my way through a shower of petals to the great trunk and for one minute stood irresolute; then, putting my foot in the broad space between the forked branches, I pulled myself up into the tree. I had some difficulty in holding on, for the branches were very large and the bark hurt my hands. But I had a delicious sense that I was doing something unusual and wonderful, so I kept climbing higher and higher, until I reached a little seat which somebody had built there so long ago that it had grown part of the tree itself. I sat there for a long, long time, feeling like a fairy on a rosy cloud. After that I spent many happy hours in my tree of paradise, thinking fair thoughts and dreaming bright dreams.

By the Window by nineteenth-century artist
Joseph Ratcliffe Skelton

SOLITUDE OF SELF

The isolation of every human soul and the necessity of self-dependence must give each individual the right to choose his own surroundings. The strongest reason for giving woman all the opportunities for higher education, for the full development of her faculties, forces of mind and body; for giving her the most enlarged freedom of thought and action; a complete emancipation from all forms of bondage, of custom, dependence, superstition; from all the crippling influences of fear, is the solitude and personal responsibility of her own individual life. The strongest reason why we ask for woman a voice in the government under which she lives; in the religion she is asked to believe; equality in social life, where she is the chief factor; a place in the trades and professions, where she may earn her bread, is because of her birthright to self-sovereignty; because, as an individual, she must rely on herself. No matter how much women prefer to lean, to be protected and supported, nor how much men desire to have them do so, they must make the voyage of life alone, and for safety in an emergency they must know something of the laws of navigation. To guide our own craft, we must be captain, pilot, engineer; with chart and compass stand at the wheel; watch the wind and waves and know when to take in the sail, and read the signs in the firmament over all. It matters not whether the solitary voyager is man or woman.

—ELIZABETH CADY STANTON, FIRST PRESIDENT
OF THE NATIONAL AMERICAN WOMAN SUFFRAGE
ASSOCIATION, FROM HER 1892 TESTIMONY BEFORE
THE CONGRESSIONAL JUDICIARY COMMITTEE

WHAT I LIVED FOR

I went to the woods because I wished to live deliberately, to front only the essential facts of life, and see if I could not learn what it had to teach, and not, when I came to die, discover that I had not lived. I did not wish to live what was not life, living is so dear; nor did I wish to practise resignation, unless it was quite necessary. I wanted to live deep and suck out all the marrow of life, to live so sturdily and Spartan-like as to put to rout all that was not life, to cut a broad swath and shave close, to drive life into a corner, and reduce it to its lowest terms, and, if it proved to be mean, why then to get the whole and genuine meanness of it, and publish its meanness to the world; or if it were sublime, to know it by experience, and be able to give a true account of it in my next excursion.

— HENRY DAVID THOREAU, FROM *WALDEN* (1854)

The First Thanksgiving Day by George Henry Boughton (1833–1905)

PILGRIMS IN THE WILDERNESS

The following account of the early experiences of Puritan settlers in seventeenth-century Massachusetts comes from William Bradford, who served as governor of Plymouth Colony from 1621 to 1651.

Being thus arrived in a good harbor, and brought safe to land, they fell upon their knees and blessed the God of heaven who had brought them over the vast and furious ocean, and delivered them from all the perils and miseries thereof, again to set their feet on the firm and stable earth, their proper element. . . .

But here I cannot but stay and make a pause, and stand half amazed at this poor people's present condition; and so I think will the reader, too, when he well considers the same. Being thus passed the vast ocean, and a sea of troubles before in their preparation . . . they had now no friends to welcome them nor inns to entertain or refresh their weather-beaten bodies; no houses or much less towns to repair to, to seek for succor.... And for the season it was winter, and they that know the winters of that country know them to be sharp and violent, and subject to cruel and fierce storms, dangerous to travel to known places, much more to search an unknown coast. Besides, what could they see but a hideous and desolate wilderness; full of wild beasts and wild men—and what multitudes there might be of them they knew not. Neither could they, as it were, go up to the top of Pisgah to view from this wilderness a more goodly country to feed their hopes; for which way soever they turned their eyes (save upward to the heavens) they could have little solace or content in respect of any outward objects. For summer being done, all things stand upon them with a weatherbeaten face, and the whole country, full of woods and thickets, represented a wild and savage hue. If they looked behind them, there was the mighty ocean which they had passed and was now as a main bar and gulf to separate them from all the civil parts of the world.

I only regret that I have but one life to lose for my country.

—THE LAST WORDS OF AMERICAN PATRIOT NATHAN HALE BEFORE HE WAS EXECUTED BY THE BRITISH IN 1776

Measured by the exertions necessary to overcome them, the difficulties that beset the modern immigrant are no less formidable than those which the Pilgrims had to face. There has never been a time when it was more difficult to get something for nothing than it is today, but the unromantic setting of modern enterprises leads us to underestimate the moral qualities that make success possible today. Undoubtedly the pioneer with an axe over his shoulder is a more picturesque figure than the clerk with a pencil behind his ear, but we who have stood up against the shocks of modern life should know better than to confuse the picturesque with the heroic. Do we not know that it takes a *man* to beat circumstances today as in the days of the pioneers?

—MARY ANTIN, FROM *THEY WHO KNOCK AT OUR GATES* (1914)

Let every nation know, whether it wishes us well or ill, that we shall pay any price, bear any burden, meet any hardship, support any friend, oppose any foe to assure the survival and the success of liberty.

—JOHN F. KENNEDY, FROM HIS 1961 INAUGURAL ADDRESS

Marine Corps Memorial, Washington, D.C.

If we take the generally accepted definition of bravery as a quality which knows not fear, I have never seen a brave man. All men are frightened. The more intelligent they are, the more they are frightened. The courageous man is the man who forces himself, in spite of his fear, to carry on. Discipline, pride, self-respect, self-confidence, and the love of glory are attributes which will make a man courageous even when he is afraid.

—GENERAL GEORGE S. PATTON, JR., FROM *WAR AS I KNEW IT* (1947)

THE INEVITABLE

I like the man who faces what he must,
    With step triumphant and a heart of cheer;
    Who fights the daily battle without fear;
Sees his hopes fail, yet keeps unfaltering trust
That God is God,—that somehow, true and just
    His plans work out for mortals; not a tear
    Is shed when fortune, which the world holds dear,
Falls from his grasp—better, with love, a crust
    Than living in dishonor: envies not,
Nor loses faith in man; but does his best,
    Nor ever murmurs at his humbler lot;
But, with a smile and words of hope, gives zest
    To every toiler: he alone is great
    Who by a life heroic conquers fate.

—SARAH KNOWLES BOLTON (1841–1916)

"I will have no man in my boat," said Starbuck, "who is not afraid of a whale." By this, he seemed to mean, not only that the most reliable and useful courage was that which arises from the fair estimation of the encountered peril, but that an utterly fearless man is a far more dangerous comrade than a coward.

—HERMAN MELVILLE (1819–1891),
FROM HIS 1851 NOVEL *MOBY DICK*

Some men see things as they are and say "Why?" I dream of things that never were and say, "Why not?"

—ROBERT KENNEDY (1925–1968)

Honesty

e have no trouble finding words to describe an honest person.

We say that he or she is truthful, or straightforward, or righteous, or reputable, or honorable—or that he or she has integrity, or gives it to you straight, or tells it like it is, or doesn't mince words. The wealth of expressions for describing honesty suggests its importance in our society.

We admire an honest person and agree with the adage that "honesty is the best policy." Yet we know that speaking the truth—or even accepting the truth—can sometimes be difficult. As writer James Russell Lowell once remarked, "No man can produce great things who is not thoroughly sincere in dealing with himself."

Often, the only consequence more difficult to endure than a painful or unpleasant truth is the consequence of not being honest in the first place. No family or business—or nation—functions well without trust, and once it is lost, it may not be so easily restored.

In the words of abolitionist William Lloyd Garrison, "In proportion as we perceive and embrace the truth do we become just, heroic, magnanimous, divine."

MANHOOD

If you would climb to the high places, carry off the richest prizes, get the most enjoyment out of life, and have the sublimest old age, you must conquer the base elements of nature; you must have every atom of the dross of dishonesty squeezed, hammered, burned out, if necessary; you must become as sound as twenty-four-karat gold, as true as the best steel. You must prove yourself as reliable as the course of nature, as incorruptible as sunlight, as pure and sweet in your personality as the breezes of Heaven. You must scorn all meanness, loathe all false pretense, be afraid of every kind of dishonesty, and hate a lie as you would hate the devil himself. You must determine stoutly to be as you appear.

There is a premium on men like that. The great world, disgusted with frauds and pretenders and shams of all kinds, will know such a man as soon as he appears. It will prize him, honor him, reward him, make him famous, and render him immortal.

—GEORGE K. MORRIS, FROM *A NOBLE LIFE AND ITS LESSONS*

All men profess honesty as long as they can. To believe all men honest would be folly. To believe none so, is something worse.

—JOHN QUINCY ADAMS
(1767–1848)

Undertake not what you cannot perform; but be careful to keep your promise.

—GEORGE WASHINGTON, FROM HIS "RULES OF CIVILITY," WRITTEN WHEN HE WAS IN HIS TEENS

Honesty pays, but it don't seem to pay enough to suit some people.

—HUMORIST F. M. HUBBARD
(1868–1930)

A MAN OF STATURE

Deerslayer, as Hurry called his companion, was a very different person in appearance, as well as in character. In stature he stood about six feet in his moccasins, but his frame was comparatively light and slender, showing muscles, however, that promised unusual agility, if not unusual strength. His face would have had little to recommend it except youth, were it not for an expression that seldom failed to win upon those who had leisure to examine it, and to yield to the feeling of confidence it created. This expression was simply that of guileless truth, sustained by an earnestness of purpose, and a sincerity of feeling, that rendered it remarkable.

At times this air of integrity seemed to be so simple as to awaken the suspicion of a want of the usual means to discriminate between artifice and truth; but few came in serious contact with the man without losing this distrust in respect for his opinions and motives.

—JAMES FENIMORE COOPER, FROM HIS 1841 NOVEL *THE DEERSLAYER*

The thing to do, when one feels sure that he has said or done the right thing, and is condemned, is to stand still and keep quiet. If he is right, time will show it.

—BOOKER T. WASHINGTON
(1856–1915)

No man can produce great things who is not thoroughly sincere in dealing with himself.

—WRITER AND DIPLOMAT
JAMES RUSSELL LOWELL
(1819–1891)

THE OX AND THE MULE

An ox and a mule worked for a farmer; they were hitched side by side to a plow and, day after day, pulled it across the fields.

One night the two came wearily back to their stable where they were fed and their stalls bedded down. The following conversation ensued.

"Mule," said the ox, "we've been working too hard recently. I'll tell you how we can get out of so much work."

"How?" asked the mule, naturally.

"It is very simple. We will play sick, and then we can lie here in our stalls all day and enjoy ourselves."

The mule, being an exceedingly intelligent creature, said, "You can do that if you choose, but I prefer to work. That is what we were meant for."

The next morning, when the farmer came out, the ox played sick. The farmer bedded him down with clean straw, gave him fresh hay, a bucket of oats and oil meal, and left him alone for the day and went forth and plowed with the mule alone.

All day the ox lay in his stall, chewing his cud and enjoying himself thoroughly. That night when the mule came in, the ox asked him how things had gone.

"It was hard and we did not get much done," said the mule.

"Did the farmer ask about me?"

"No," replied the mule. "He did not speak of you."

"Well, then," said the ox, pleased with his cleverness, "I think I'll play sick again tomorrow. It's exceedingly pleasant to lie here and rest and have my food brought to me. I don't know why I didn't think of this long ago."

"I think," said the mule, "I'll go back to work tomorrow as usual."

So the ox played [sick] again and lay in his stall and lived on choice food.

That night, when the mule came in, the ox again inquired how things had gone.

"About the same as yesterday," answered the mule.

"Did the farmer say anything about me?" asked the ox.

"Yes, he did," said the mule. "It chanced, as we came to the end of the plow row, a butcher drove by and stopped and asked the farmer if he had an animal he would sell. 'Yes, I have,' said the farmer. 'I have an ox I would like to dispose of.' The butcher agreed and drove on and that was the end of the conversation," said the mule, beginning to eat his oats.

—From *Treasury of American Anecdotes* (B.A. Botkin, 1957)

I hope I shall always possess firmness and virtue enough to maintain what I consider the most enviable of all titles, the character of an honest man.

—George Washington
(1732–1799)

In proportion as we perceive and embrace the truth do we become just, heroic, magnanimous, divine.

—Abolitionist William Lloyd Garrison (1805–1879)

FROM BOY TO MAN

There is no need for a boy to preach about his own good conduct and virtue. If he does he will make himself offensive and ridiculous. But there is urgent need that he should practice decency; that he should be clean and straight, honest and truthful, gentle and tender, as well as brave. If he can once get to a proper understanding of things, he will have a far more hearty contempt for the boy who has begun a course of feeble dissipation, or who is untruthful, or mean, or dishonest, or cruel, than this boy and his fellows can possibly, in return, feel for him. The very fact that the boy should be manly and able to hold his own, that he should be ashamed to submit to bullying without instant retaliation, should, in return, make him abhor any form of bullying, cruelty, or brutality.

The boy can best become a good man by being a good boy—not a goody-goody boy, but just a plain good boy. I do not mean that he must love only the negative virtues; I mean he must love the positive virtues also. "Good," in the largest sense, should include whatever is fine, straightforward, clean, brave, and manly.

—THEODORE ROOSEVELT (1858–1919), FROM HIS ESSAY "THE AMERICAN BOY"

THE CHILD WITHIN

In this kingdom of illusions we grope eagerly for stays and foundations. There is none but a strict and faithful dealing at home, and a severe barring out of all duplicity or illusion there. Whatever games are played with us, we must play no games with ourselves, but deal in our privacy with the last honesty and truth. I look upon the simple and childish virtues of veracity and honesty as the root of all that is sublime in character. Speak as you think, be what you are, pay your debts of all kinds. I prefer to be [known] as sound and solvent, and my word as good as my bond, and to be what cannot be skipped, or dissipated, or undermined, to all the *éclat* in the universe. This reality is the foundation of friendship, religion, poetry, and art. At the top or at the bottom of all illusions, I set the cheat which still leads us to work and live for appearances, in spite of our conviction, in all sane hours, that it is what we really are that avails with friends, with strangers, and with fate or fortune.

—RALPH WALDO EMERSON,
FROM *THE CONDUCT OF LIFE* (1860)

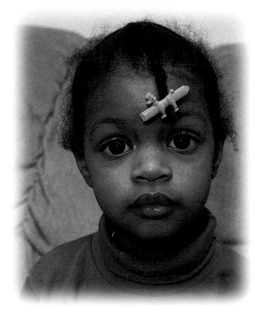

THOUGHTS ON BENEDICT ARNOLD'S BETRAYAL

When we take a review of the history of former times it will turn out to the honor of America that, notwithstanding the trying variety of her situation, this is the only instance of defection in a general officer; and even in this case, the unshaken honesty of those who detected him heightens the national character, to which his apostasy serves as a foil. From the nature of his crime, and his disposition to monopolize, it is reasonable to conclude he had few or no direct accomplices. His sole object was to make a monied bargain; and to be consistent with himself, he would as readily betray the side he has deserted to, as that he deserted from.

But there is one reflection [that] results from this black business that deserves notice, which is that it shows the declining power of the enemy. An attempt to bribe is a sacrifice of military fame, and a confession of inability to conquer; as a proud people they ought to be above it, and as soldiers to despise it; and however they may feel on the occasion, the world at large will despise them for it, and consider America superior to their arms.

—PHILOSOPHER AND AUTHOR THOMAS PAINE (1737–1809)

Lewis & Clark Expedition by Oscar Edmund Berninghaus (1874–1952)

In a letter dated August 18, 1813, Thomas Jefferson gave the following assessment of Meriwether Lewis, who had worked for him for two years before being appointed co-leader of the so-called Lewis & Clark Expedition (1804–1806).

Captain Lewis, who had then been near two years with me as private secretary, immediately renewed his solicitations to have the direction of the party. I had now had opportunities of knowing him intimately. Of courage undaunted; possessing a firmness and perseverance of purpose which nothing but impossibilities could divert from its direction; careful as a father of those committed to his charge, yet steady in the maintenance of order and discipline; intimate with the Indian character, customs, and principles; habituated to the hunting life; guarded, by exact observation of the vegetables and animals of his own country, against losing time in the description of objects already possessed; honest, disinterested, liberal, of sound understanding, and a fidelity to truth so scrupulous, that whatever he should report would be as certain as if seen by ourselves; with all these qualifications, as if selected and implanted by nature in one body for this express purpose, I could have no hesitation in confiding the enterprise to him.

WHO STOLE THE BIRD'S NEST?

Early twentieth-century readers often contained moral lessons. In this poem, by Lydia Maria Child, the animals serve as teachers.

"To-whit! to-whit! to-whee!
Will you listen to me?
Who stole four eggs I laid,
And the nice nest I made?"

"Not I," said the cow, "Moo-oo!
Such a thing I'd never do.
I gave you a wisp of hay,
But didn't take your nest away.
Not I," said the cow, "Moo-oo!
Such a thing I'd never do."

"To-whit! to-whit! to-whee!
Will you listen to me?
Who stole four eggs I laid,
And the nice nest I made?"

"Bob-o'-link! Bob-o'-link!
Now what do you think?
Who stole a nest away
From the plum-tree, to-day?"

"Not I," said the dog, "Bow-wow!
I wouldn't be so mean, I vow!
I gave hairs for the nest to make,
But the nest I did not take.
Not I," said the dog, "Bow-wow!
I'm not so mean, anyhow."

"To-whit! to-whit! to-whee!
Will you listen to me?
Who stole four eggs I laid,
And the nice nest I made?"

"Bob-o'-link! Bob-o'-link!
Now what do you think?
Who stole a nest away
From the plum-tree, to-day?"

"Coo-coo! Coo-coo! Coo-coo!
Let me speak a word, too!
Who stole that pretty nest
From little yellow-breast?"

"Not I," said the sheep, "Oh, no!
I wouldn't treat a poor bird so.
I gave wool the nest to line,
But the nest was none of mine.
Baa! Baa!" said the sheep, "Oh, no!
I wouldn't treat a poor bird so."

"To-whit! to-whit! to-whee!
Will you listen to me?
Who stole four eggs I laid,
And the nice nest I made?"

"Bob-o'-link! Bob-o'-link!
Now what do you think?
Who stole a nest away
From the plum-tree, to-day?"

"Coo-coo! Coo-coo! Coo-coo!
Let me speak a word, too!
Who stole that pretty nest
From little yellow-breast?"

"Caw! Caw!" cried the crow;
"I should like to know
What thief took away
A bird's nest to-day?"

"Cluck! Cluck!" said the hen;
"Don't ask me again,
Why I haven't a chick
Would do such a trick.
We all gave her a feather,
And she wove them together.
I'd scorn to intrude
On her and her brood.
Cluck! Cluck!" said the hen,
"Don't ask me again."

"Chirr-a-whirr! Chirr-a-whirr!
All the birds make a stir!
Let us find out his name,
And all cry 'For shame!'"

A little boy hung down his head,
And went and hid behind the bed,
For he stole that pretty nest
From poor little yellow-breast.
And he felt so full of shame,
He didn't like to tell his name.

THE YANKEE IN SEARCH OF ADVENTURES

Perhaps the ultimate "fish out of water" story, A Connecticut Yankee in King Arthur's Court *(1889), by Mark Twain, contrasts nineteenth-century American standards of truth and order with those of Europe in the Middle Ages.*

There never was such a country for wandering liars; and they were of both sexes. Hardly a month went by without one of these tramps arriving; and generally loaded with a tale about some princess or other wanting help to get her out of some far-away castle where she was held in captivity by a lawless scoundrel, usually a giant. Now you would think that the first thing the king would do after listening to such a novelette from an entire stranger, would be to ask for credentials—yes, and a pointer or two as to locality of castle, best route to it, and so-on. But nobody ever thought of so simple and common-sense a thing as that. No, everybody swallowed those people's lies whole, and never asked a question of any sort or about anything. Well, one day when I was not around, one of these people came along—it was a she one, this time—and told a tale of the usual pattern. Her mistress was a captive in a vast and gloomy castle, along with forty-four other young and beautiful girls, pretty much all of them princesses; they had been languishing in that cruel captivity for twenty-six years; the masters of the castle were three stupendous brothers, each with four arms and one eye—the eye in the centre of the forehead, and as big as a fruit. Sort of fruit not mentioned; their usual slovenliness in statistics.

Would you believe it?—the king and the whole Round Table were in raptures over this preposterous opportunity for adventure. Every knight of the Table jumped for the chance, and begged for it; but to their vexation and chagrin the king conferred it upon me, who had not asked for it at all.

Original woodcut depicting Mark Twain's "Connecticut Yankee"

By an effort, I contained my joy when Clarence brought me the news. But he—he could not contain his. His mouth gushed delight and gratitude in a steady discharge—delight in my good fortune, gratitude to the king for this splendid mark of his favor for me. He could keep neither his legs nor his body still, but pirouetted about the place in an airy ecstasy of happiness.

On my side, I could have cursed the kindness that conferred upon me this benefaction, but I kept my vexation under the surface for policy's sake, and did what I could to let on to be glad. Indeed, I *said* I was glad. And in a way, it was true: I was as glad as a person is when he is scalped.

Well, one must take the best of things, and not waste time with useless fretting, but get down to business and see what can be done. In all lies there is wheat among the chaff; I must get at the wheat in this case: so I sent for the girl, and she came. She was a comely enough creature, and soft and modest, but if signs went for anything, she didn't know as much as a lady's watch. I said—

"My dear, have you been questioned as to particulars?" She said she hadn't.

"Well, I didn't expect you had, but I thought I would ask, to make sure; it's the way I've been raised. Now you mustn't take it unkindly if I remind you that as we don't know you, we must go a little slow. You may be all right, of course, and we'll hope that you are; but to take it for granted isn't business. *You* understand that. I'm obliged to ask you a few questions; just answer up fair and square, and don't be afraid. Where do you live, when you are at home?"

"In the land of Moder, fair sir."

"Land of Moder. I don't remember hearing of it before. Parents living?"

"As to that, I know not if they be yet on live, sith it is many years that I have lain shut up in the castle."

"Your name, please?"

"I hight the Demoiselle Alisande la Carteloise, an it please you."

"Do you know anybody here who can identify you?"

"That were not likely, fair lord, I being come hither now for the first time."

"Have you brought any letters—any documents—any proofs that you are trustworthy and truthful?"

"Of a surety, no; and wherefore should I? Have I not a tongue, and cannot I say all that myself?"

"But your saying it, you know, and somebody else's saying it, is different."

If a man does not keep pace with his companions, perhaps it is because he hears a different drummer. Let him keep step to music which he hears, however measured or far away.

—HENRY DAVID THOREAU (1817–1862)

REAL POWER

Wealth is power, talent is power, and knowledge is power. But there is a mightier force in the world than any of these—a power which wealth is not rich enough to purchase, nor talent strong enough to overcome, nor knowledge wise enough to overreach; all these tremble in its presence. It is truth—the most potent element in our social and individual life.

Though tossed upon the billows of popular commotion, or cast into the seven-fold furnace of persecution, or trampled into the dust by the iron heel of power, truth is the one indestructible thing in this world, that loses in no conflict, suffers from no misusage and abuse, and maintains its vitality and completeness after every reverse. All kinds of conspiracies have been exhausted to crush it, and all kinds of plans laid to vitiate and poison it; but none has succeeded, and none ever will. We can be confident of nothing else in this world but the safety and imperishability of truth—for it is part of the Divine nature, and invested with the character of its author.

It may often seem to be in danger; it is as much set upon and assaulted now as ever, but history and experience ought to reassure our faith. It has never yet failed, and it never will. It has always accomplished its end, and always will. We may rest serenely upon it, and feel no alarm; we may anticipate its success, and enjoy its triumphs in advance. In this struggling life, what encouragement and comfort is there in this thought—that the man of truth and the cause of truth have the certainty of success; they cannot fail. "Truth crushed to earth will rise again." It cannot be put down.

—ANONYMOUS

BOY WANTED

Attributed to Frank Crane (1861–1939), a clergyman and syndicated writer of inspirational columns, this "want ad" began appearing in newspapers around the turn of the century.

Wanted—A boy that stands straight, sits straight, acts straight, and talks straight; . . .

A boy who, when he does not know a thing, says, "I don't know," and when he has made a mistake says, "I'm sorry," and when he is asked to do a thing says, "I'll try";

A boy who looks you right in the eye and tells the truth every time; . . .

A boy who would rather lose his job or be expelled from school than to tell a lie or be a cad; . . .

This boy is wanted everywhere. The family wants him, the school wants him, the office wants him, the boys want him, the girls want him, all creation wants him.

A great business is seldom if ever built up, except on lines of the strictest integrity. A reputation for "cuteness" and sharp dealing is fatal in great affairs. Not the letter of the law, but the spirit, must be the rule. The standard of commercial morality is now very high. A mistake made by any one in favor of the firm is corrected as promptly as if the error were in favor of the other party. It is essential to permanent success that a house should obtain a reputation for being governed by what is fair rather than what is merely legal. A rule which we adopted and adhered to has given greater returns than one would believe possible, namely: always give the other party the benefit of the doubt.

—INDUSTRIALIST ANDREW CARNEGIE (1835–1919)

What I must do is all that concerns me, not what the people think. This rule, equally arduous in actual and in intellectual life, may serve for the whole distinction between greatness and meanness. It is the harder because you will always find those who think they know what is your duty better than you know it. It is easy in the world to live after the world's opinion; it is easy in solitude to live after your own; but the great man is he who in the midst of the crowd keeps with perfect sweetness the independence of solitude.

—RALPH WALDO EMERSON (1803–1882)

THE YOUNG STOREKEEPER

A RETELLING BY AUTHOR HORATIO ALGER (1832–1899)

As a clerk Abraham Lincoln proved honest and efficient, and my readers will be interested in some illustrations of the former trait which I find in Dr. Holland's interesting volume.

One day a woman came into the store and purchased sundry articles. They footed up two dollars and six and a quarter cents, or the young clerk thought they did. We do not hear nowadays of six and a quarter cents, but this was a coin borrowed from the Spanish currency, and was well known in my own boyhood.

The bill was paid, and the woman was entirely satisfied. But the young storekeeper, not feeling quite sure as to the accuracy of his calculation, added up the items once more. To his dismay he found that the sum total should have been but two dollars.

"I've made her pay six and a quarter cents too much," said Abe, disturbed.

It was a trifle, and many clerks would have dismissed it as such. But Abe was too conscientious for that.

"The money must be paid back," he decided.

This would have been easy enough had the woman lived "just round the corner," but, as the young man knew, she lived between two and three miles away. This, however, did not alter the matter. It was night, but he closed and locked the store, and walked to the residence of his customer. Arrived there, he explained the matter, paid over the six and a quarter cents, and returned satisfied. If I were a capitalist, I would be willing to lend money to such a young man without security.

In a letter to Dr. Walter Jones dated January 2, 1814, Thomas Jefferson gave the following appraisal of George Washington, whom he had known for many years before his death in 1799.

I think I knew General Washington intimately and thoroughly; and were I called on to delineate his character, it should be in terms like these.

His mind was great and powerful, without being of the very first order; his penetration strong, though not so acute as that of a Newton, Bacon, or Locke; and as far as he saw, no judgment was ever sounder. It was slow in operation, being little aided by invention or imagination, but sure in conclusion. Hence the common remark of his officers, of the advantage he derived from councils of war, where hearing all suggestions, he selected whatever was best; and certainly no general ever planned his battles more judiciously. But if deranged during the course of the action, if any member of his plan was dislocated by sudden circumstances, he was slow in readjustment. The consequence was, that he often failed in the field and rarely against an enemy in station, as at Boston and York.

He was incapable of fear, meeting personal dangers with the calmest unconcern. Perhaps the strongest feature in his character was prudence, never acting until every circumstance, every consideration, was maturely weighed; refraining if he saw a doubt, but, when once decided, going through with his purpose, whatever obstacles opposed. His integrity was most pure, his justice the most inflexible I have ever known, no motives of interest or consanguinity, of friendship or hatred, being able to bias his decision. He was, indeed, in every sense of the words, a wise, a good, and a great man.

His temper was naturally irritable and high toned; but reflection and resolution had obtained a firm and habitual ascendancy over it. If ever, however, it broke its bonds, he was most tremendous in his wrath. In his expenses he was honorable, but exact; liberal in contributions to whatever promised utility; but frowning and unyielding on all visionary projects, and all unworthy calls on his charity.

Portrait of George Washington by John Trumbull (1756–1843)

Compassion

Americans have made heroes of the rugged individuals who forged a country out of the wilderness, but they particularly revered those who exhibited compassion in their dealings with other people.

More than half a century before American independence was achieved, Puritan clergyman Cotton Mather was encouraging colonists to help neighbors who were ill or in despair. "Visit them," he pleaded, "and when you visit them, comfort them. Carry them some good word which may raise a gladness in a heart stooping with heaviness."

The helping hand is a central image in American history. For the millions of immigrants who arrived in this country by way of New York harbor, American compassion has been artfully symbolized by the Statue of Liberty. "Give me your tired, your poor, your huddled masses yearning to breathe free," says the famous poem by Emma Lazarus that is anchored to the statue's pedestal. "Send these, the homeless, tempest-tost to me; I lift my lamp beside the golden door!"

As "New Deal" President Franklin Delano Roosevelt once put it, the test of our progress as a nation "is not whether we add more to the abundance of those who have much; it is whether we provide enough for those who have too little."

Boys are better capable of governing themselves than of submitting to government by adults. Don't repress a boy, give him outlets for his energies. Don't preach at him, give him the example you want him to follow. Make him responsible. Remember, *there are no bad boys.*

—Fr. Edward Joseph Flanagan (1886–1948), founder of
Father Flanagan's Boys Home in Boys Town, Nebraska

Sympatica is the touchstone that leads to talent's highest altitude.

—Minna Antrim (1861–?)

When we listen to "the better angels of our nature," we find that they celebrate the simple things, the basic things—such as goodness, decency, love, kindness. Greatness comes in simple trappings.

—Richard M. Nixon, from his 1969 Inaugural Address

Sirs, would it be too much for you at least once in a week to think: "What neighbor is reduced into a pinching and painful poverty? Or in any degree impoverished with heavy losses?" Think: "What neighbor is languishing with sickness, especially if sick with sore maladies and of some continuance?" Think: "What neighbor is heartbroken with sad bereavements, bereaved of desirable relative?" And think: "What neighbor has a soul buffeted and hurried with violent assaults of the wicked one?" But then think: "What shall be done for such neighbors?"

First: You will pity them. The evangelical precept is: "Have compassion one of another—be pitiful." It was of old, and ever will be, the just expectation: "To him that is afflicted, pity should be shown." And let our pity to them flame out in our prayer for

them. It were a very lovely practice for you, in the daily prayer of your closet every evening, to think: "What miserable object have I seen today that I may do well now to mention for the mercies of the Lord?"

But this is not all. 'Tis possible, 'tis probable, you may do well to visit them: and when you visit them, comfort them. Carry them some good word which may raise a gladness in an heart stooping with heaviness.

And lastly: give them all the assistances that may answer their occasions. Assist them with advice to them, assist them with address to others for them. And if it be needful, bestow your alms upon them. . . .

—CLERGYMAN AND AUTHOR COTTON MATHER (1663–1728); FROM *THE AMERICAN PURITANS: THEIR PROSE AND POETRY* (ANCHOR BOOKS, 1956)

OJIBWAY PRAYER

Grandfather,
Look at our brokenness.

We know that in all creation
Only the human family
Has strayed from the Sacred Way.
We know that we are the ones
Who are divided,
And we are the ones
Who must come back together
To walk the Sacred Way.
Grandfather,
Sacred One,
Teach us love, compassion,
*   and honor*
That we may heal the earth
And heal each other.

Compassion [is] the fairest associate of the heart.

—THOMAS PAINE (1737–1809)

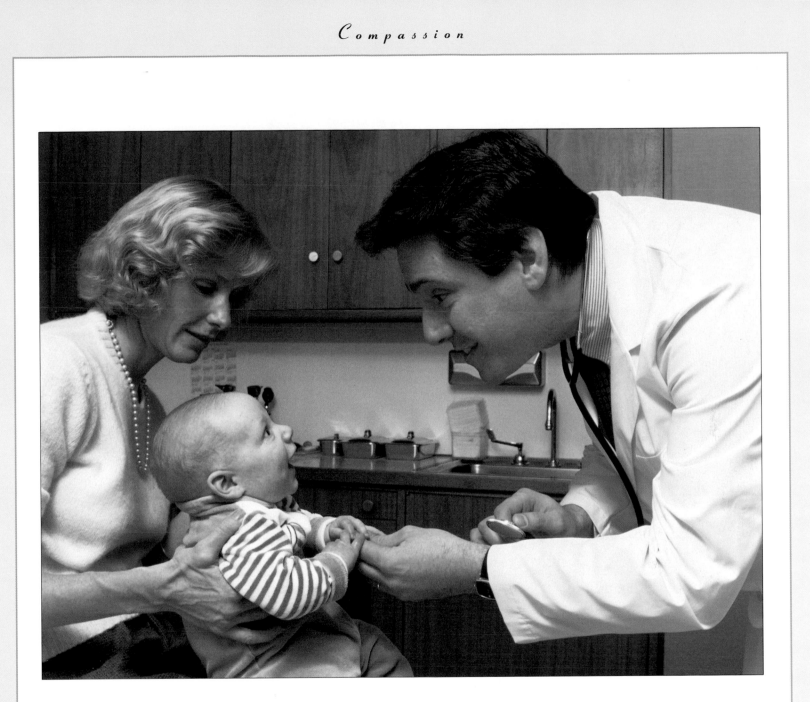

Compassion will cure more than condemnation.

—AMERICAN PROVERB

Little deeds of kindness,
Little words of love,
Help to make earth happy
Like the heaven above.

—JULIA A. FLETCHER CARNEY
(1823–1908), FROM "LITTLE
THINGS" (1845)

[leave] to boys, jointly, all the idle fields and commons where ball may be played, all pleasant waters where one may swim, all snow-clad hills where one may coast, and all streams and ponds where one may fish, or where, when winter comes, one may skate, to have and to hold the same for the period of their boyhood. And all the meadows, with clover blossoms and butterflies thereof, the woods with their appurtenances, the birds and squirrels and echoes and strange noises, and all distant places which may be visited, together with the adventures there to be found.

—FROM THE WILL OF CHARLES LOUNSBURY, A NEBRASKA LAWYER
WHO BEQUEATHED THE LAND THAT BECAME BOYS TOWN IN 1917

*We have a great deal more kindness
than is ever spoken.*

—RALPH WALDO EMERSON (1803–1882)

THE NEW COLOSSUS

This famous poem, by Emma Lazarus (1849–1887), is engraved on a tablet attached to the pedestal of the Statue of Liberty.

Not like the brazen giant of Greek fame,
With conquering limbs astride from land to land;
Here at our sea-washed, sunset gates shall stand
A mighty woman with a torch, whose flame
Is the imprisoned lightning, and her name
Mother of Exiles. From her beacon-hand
Glows world-wide welcome; her mild eyes command
The air-bridged harbor that twin cities frame.
"Keep ancient lands, your storied pomp!" cries she
With silent lips. "Give me your tired, your poor,
Your huddled masses yearning to breathe free,
The wretched refuse of your teeming shore.
Send these, the homeless, tempest-tost to me,
I lift my lamp beside the golden door!"

Because of what America is and what America has done, a firmer courage, a higher hope, inspires the heart of all humanity.

—CALVIN COOLIDGE (1872–1933)

We would like to see more small communities organizing themselves, people talking with people, people *caring* for people, people coming together in order to make known what they believe and what they would like their nation to do.... We believe we are doing what our Founding Fathers came here to do, to worship God in the communities they settled. They were farmers. They were craftspeople. They took care of each other. They prayed to God, and they thanked Him for showing them the way—to America!

—DOROTHY DAY, FROM *DOROTHY DAY: A RADICAL DEVOTION*
BY ROBERT COLES (ADDISON-WESLEY, 1987)

ars of extermination, engaged in by people pursuing commerce and all industrial pursuits, are expensive even against the weakest people, and are demoralizing and wicked. Our superiority of strength and advantages of civilization should make us lenient toward the Indian. The wrong inflicted upon him should be taken into account and the balance placed to his credit. The moral view of the question should be considered and the question asked, Can not the Indian be made a useful and productive member of society by proper teaching and treatment? If the effort is made in good faith, we will stand better before the civilized nations of the earth and in our own consciences for having made it.

—ULYSSES S. GRANT, FROM HIS 1873 INAUGURAL ADDRESS

Compassion is not weakness, and concern for the unfortunate is not socialism.

—HUBERT H. HUMPHREY
(1911–1978)

POCAHONTAS

Upon the barren sand
　A single captive stood;
Around him came, with bow and brand,
　The red men of the wood.
Like him of old, his doom he hears,
　Rock-bound on ocean's brim —
The chieftain's daughter knelt in tears,
　And breathed a prayer for him.

Above his head in air
　The savage war-club swung:
The frantic girl, in wild despair,
　Her arms about him flung.
Then shook the warriors of the shade,
　Like leaves on aspen limb,
Subdued by that heroic maid
　Who breathed a prayer for him!

"Unbind him!" gasped the chief:
　"It is your king's decree!"
He kiss'd away the tears of grief,
　And set the captive free!
'T is ever thus, when in life's storm
　Hope's star to man grows dim,
An angel kneels, in woman's form,
　And breathes a prayer for him.

—JOURNALIST AND POET GEORGE POPE
　MORRIS (1802–1864); FROM *POEMS OF
　AMERICAN HISTORY* (HOUGHTON MIFFLIN
　COMPANY, 1950)

Participants in the 1986 "Hands Across America" charity campaign near Clines Corner, New Mexico.

As long as there is one upright man, as long as there is one compassionate woman, the contagion may spread and the scene is not desolate. Hope is the thing that is left to us, in a bad time.

—JOURNALIST AND WRITER E. B. WHITE (1899–1985),
FROM A LETTER DATED MARCH 30, 1973

Friend of the poor!—go on—
   Speak for the Truth and Right!
Onward—though hate and scorn
   Gloom round thee as the night.
Speak—at each word of thine,
   Some ancient Fraud is riven,
And through its rents of ruin shine
   The sunbeams and the heaven!

—JOHN G. WHITTIER (1807–1892),
KNOWN AS "THE QUAKER POET"

I see millions of families trying to live on incomes so meager that the pall of family disaster hangs over them day by day.

I see millions whose daily lives in city and on farm continue under conditions labeled indecent by a so-called polite society half a century ago.

I see millions denied education, recreation, and the opportunity to better their lot and the lot of their children.

I see millions lacking the means to buy the products of farm and factory and by their poverty denying work and productiveness to many other millions.

I see one-third of a nation ill-housed, ill-clad, ill-nourished.

It is not in despair that I paint you that picture. I paint it for you in hope—because the Nation, seeing and understanding the injustice in it, proposes to paint it out. We are determined to make every American citizen the subject of his country's interest and concern; and we will never regard any faithful law-abiding group within our borders as superfluous. The test of our progress is not whether we add more to the abundance of those who have much; it is whether we provide enough for those who have too little.

—FRANKLIN DELANO ROOSEVELT (1882–1945)

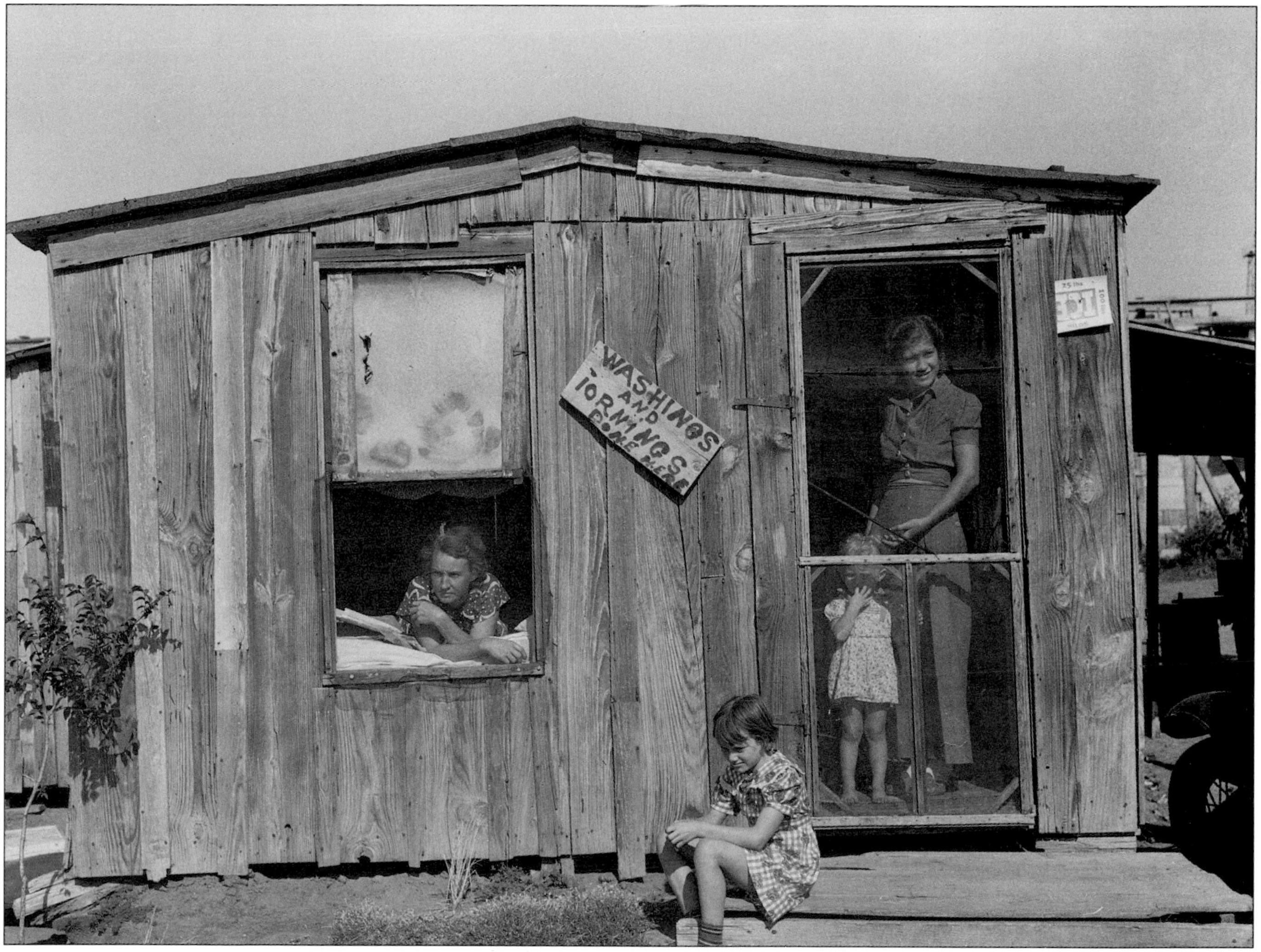
WASHINGS
AND
IORNINGS

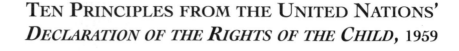

TEN PRINCIPLES FROM THE UNITED NATIONS' *DECLARATION OF THE RIGHTS OF THE CHILD*, 1959

1. All children, without regard to race, color, sex, language, religion, political or other opinion, national or social origin, property, birth, or other status, are entitled to the rights set out in the Declaration of the Rights of the Child, adopted by the United Nations, 1959.

2. The child shall enjoy special protection and be given opportunities and facilities to develop physically, mentally, morally, spiritually, and socially.

3. The child shall be entitled to a name and nationality.

4. The child shall have the right to adequate nutrition, housing, recreational, and medical services.

5. The child who is physically, mentally, or socially handicapped shall be given special treatment, education, and care.

6. Wherever possible, the child should grow up with its parents. Society and public authorities have the duty to extend special care to children without a family and means of support.

7. The child is entitled to free and compulsory education. The child shall have the opportunity for play and recreation.

8. The child shall always be among the first to receive protection and relief.

9. The child shall be protected from all forms of neglect, cruelty, and exploitation. Child labor shall not be allowed.

10. The child shall be protected from practices which foster discrimination in any form. The child shall be brought up in a spirit of understanding, tolerance, friendship among peoples, peace, and universal brotherhood.